Sublime

2025

Sublime
adjective
1. of the most very great excellence or beauty
2. (of a persons attitude or behaviour) extreme or unparalleled

Subliminal
1. below the threshold of consciousness; perceived by or affecting someone's mind without their being aware of it.

Sublime: A daily journal for gentle, positive growth, self-love and balance
Copyright © 2024 K High.
All rights reserved.
ISBN: 978-1-7637999-0-5

Connect with me on socials @familyhypnotherapy
email kim@familyhypnotherapy.com.au

I would like to acknowledge the Traditional owners of the land on which I live, work, & create, the Wadawurrung people. I pay my respect to their elders past & present. I express my gratitude for living on this land. I love the trees & paths that lead to peaceful moments in the bush. I feel the soft sand under my feet holding my every step. I smell & taste the fresh salty air & hear the wind through the dune grasses, it clears my busy mind. I see the green bush for miles & miles. My heart smiles at this beautiful life.

just for you:

This Journal is Just For You

This journal offers daily prompts to lift your mindset & promote personal growth & self love from a subconscious level. Choose to respond to the words that make your heart smile & that offer you growth in self-reflection.

As a hypnotherapist, I have encouraged the power of visualisation & positive reflection throughout. Feel free to draw when writing does not feel right, or cut & paste, or name a song, or...?
this is your space.

**Each month has a breathing or thought technique - please use these mindfully & stop if you are feeling strain, overwhelm or find the practice triggering for you.

This Message From Me

May you know that they are whispering, "you are lovely" when they have been in your company.
May you feel your goodness overshadow your doubt & second guessing.
May the shimmers of the path you are on remind you that you are where you need to be.
May you see yourself as I do - exactly as you are, exactly enough, whole & doing the best job in this moment.

Kim

How to use this Journal

Daily Prompts

3 morning & 3 evening prompts encourage healthy, loving thoughts for you. You may find some don't feel right for your day & you would prefer to use a previous prompt, or your own, please do...

There is no pressure here - this is your space.

Morning

<u>PRESENCE</u> - These prompts are for reflection after a moment of stillness in the early morning. Close your eyes & take some gentle breaths, use the prompt to direct your morning thoughts.

<u>INTENTION</u> - This space is to plant a seed into your day of the kinds of thoughts, responses & feelings you would like to visualise into your day.

<u>RESOURCES</u> - Bring focus to what you know about your capabilities & strengths, reflect on the way they can support your day ahead.

Evening

<u>POSITIVES</u> - With some gratitude practice & some positive reflection. Frame the good in the day that has passed.

<u>CHALLENGES</u> - Gathering learning experience gained from everyday challenges & acknowledging the difficulties presented and overcome.

<u>KINDNESS</u> - Reflections on and intentions set for your journey to self-kindness.

Weekly R & R

<u>REFLECT & REFOCUS</u> - Tie your experience together to promote growth & motivation. Reflect on the week that has passed & refocus on the week ahead.

Monthly Visualisations

A guided visualisation prompt to help you stay aligned with your best vision of a balanced & fulfilled self.

Write, draw, paste clippings and quotes...

Words for You

Highlight the affirmations that feel right for you, or close your eyes and let your finger land on one to use today!

Self-Love & Self-Worth:

- I am worthy of love & respect.
- I love & accept myself unconditionally.
- My self-worth is not determined by others' opinions.
- I am enough just as I am.
- I deserve happiness & success.
- I am proud of the person I am becoming.
- I am worthy of all the good in my life.
- My imperfections make me unique & beautiful.
- I love my body & trust its wisdom.
- I am confident in my abilities & strengths.

Confidence & Inner Strength:

- I am strong, capable, & resilient.
- I believe in myself
- I trust myself to make the best decisions.
- My confidence grows with each step I take.
- I am courageous & stand up for myself.
- I embrace challenges as opportunities to grow.
- My mind is filled with positive, healthy, & loving thoughts.
- I am in charge of how I feel.
- I have the power to create the life I desire.
- My potential is limitless.

Overcoming Fear & Self-Doubt:

- I release all self-doubt & embrace my inner strength.
- I release the need to compare myself to others.
- I am brave, bold, & beautiful.
- I am proud of all the progress I've made.
- I let go of fear & have faith in myself.
- I trust my journey & know I am on the right path.
- I am not afraid to step out of my comfort zone.
- My inner light shines bright, no matter the circumstances.
- I rise above self-doubt & embrace my full potential.

Gratitude & Contentment:

- I am grateful for my body & all it does for me.
- I embrace all the love & happiness that life has to offer.
- I am grateful for the abundance in my life.
- My heart is full of gratitude & love.
- I appreciate & value everything I have.
- I attract positive energy & abundant opportunities.
- I am grateful for the lessons I learn from challenges.
- My heart is full of compassion, gratitude, & love.

January

Fresh Beginnings & New Intentions

As the new year begins & summer is in full swing, visualise yourself standing at the start of a fresh journey. Imagine the warmth of the sun energising you, filling you with confidence & optimism. Picture the intentions you want to set for the year ahead: What are your priorities for health, career, relationships, & personal growth? See yourself moving forward with clarity & enthusiasm, knowing that you have everything you need to create a fulfilling year. Describe how these intentions look, feel, taste, sound...

1. Wednesday

PRESENCE: Three thoughts that are present for me this morning:

_____
_____
_____

INTENTION: The times/places where I will remember to remain calm in my mind today:

_____
_____
_____

RESOURCES: Which of my personal strengths could be my focus today?

_____
_____
_____

POSITIVES: What was a moment today that made me feel proud of myself?

_____
_____
_____

CHALLENGES: How did I initially respond to the biggest challenge of my day?

_____
_____
_____

KINDNESS: What is one kind thing I did for myself today?

_____
_____
_____

2. Thursday

PRESENCE: What sensations do I notice in my body this morning?

_____

_____

INTENTION: In what ways can I treat myself with kindness today?

_____

_____

RESOURCES: Is there a change I can embrace for growth today?

_____

_____

POSITIVES: What am I grateful for in my health or well-being?

_____

_____

CHALLENGES: A challenge I can reframe as an opportunity to develop new skills:

_____

_____

KINDNESS: How can I practice more self-compassion when I make mistakes?

_____

_____

3. Friday

PRESENCE: What emotions am I experiencing this morning? (&allow them to just be)

___

___

___

INTENTION: What can I embrace about myself without judgement today?

___

___

___

RESOURCES: I can stay grounded in my strength through these challenges today?

___

___

___

POSITIVES: What is one task or goal I completed today that I'm proud of?

___

___

___

CHALLENGES: An obstacle I encountered today, & how I overcame it:

___

___

___

KINDNESS: What negative self-talk did I notice today, & how can I flip it to self-love?

___

___

___

4. Saturday

PRESENCE: What can I hear in this moment, right now?

INTENTION: How can I honor my boundaries & personal limits today?

RESOURCES: In what way can I use my knowledge of my self to make intentional choices today?

POSITIVES: One thing I'm grateful for that contributed to my peace of mind today.

CHALLENGES: What mistake did I make today & what did I learn from it?

KINDNESS: What can I unconditionally accept about myself as I am today?

---

5. Sunday

PRESENCE: What can I see in the space around me right now?

INTENTION: Where can I release some need for control today & let myself go with the flow?

RESOURCES: I can allow these thoughts & emotions I am noticing, without judgment:

POSITIVES: One way I demonstrated personal strength today.

CHALLENGES: How did I manage stress today? What worked well for me?

KINDNESS: What positives did I tell myself, & how did it affect my mood?

R & R

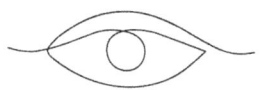

REFLECT
What was the most fulfilling moment of the past week, & why did it stand out to you?

_____
_____
_____
_____
_____
_____
_____
_____

REFOCUS
Where can you create more fulfilling moments like these in the week ahead?

_____
_____
_____
_____
_____
_____
_____
_____

6. Monday

PRESENCE: What distractions are pulling me away from the present moment right now, & how can I let them go?

_____
_____
_____

INTENTION: In what ways can I practice patience with myself today?

_____
_____
_____

RESOURCES: How can I balance my desire for growth with the need to be kind to myself today?

_____
_____
_____

POSITIVES: What is something I did today that I feel proud & thankful for?

_____
_____
_____

CHALLENGES: What strength did I rely on to get through challenges today?

_____
_____
_____

KINDNESS: How did I take care of my emotional well-being today, & how can I continue to do so?

_____
_____
_____

7. Tuesday

PRESENCE: Which tasks can I approach today with presence & awareness?

___

INTENTION: How can I show myself love & care today?

___

RESOURCES: How can I maintain a sense of inner calm today, while also leaning into my strengths?

___

POSITIVES: How did I feel connected to others in a meaningful way today?

___

CHALLENGES: A challenge today that allowed me to practice my problem-solving skills.

___

KINDNESS: What did I do today that made me feel proud of myself?

8. Wednesday

PRESENCE: With eyes closed, my mind feels...

_____
_____

INTENTION: Where in my day can I quiet the inner critic & trust myself more?

_____
_____

RESOURCES: Which challenges today can I respond to with more awareness & mindfulness?

_____
_____
_____

POSITIVES: What is one thing about my life today that brings me peace or comfort?

_____
_____

CHALLENGES: How were my challenges important to my personal growth?

_____
_____

KINDNESS: How can I show kindness to myself when I make a mistake?

_____
_____

9. Thursday

PRESENCE: Focusing on the rhythm of my breath, how does it feel?

INTENTION: What can I do today to feel more balanced & centred?

RESOURCES: How can I use my self awareness to approach today with more clarity?

POSITIVES: What is one thing I accomplished today, big or small, that I am proud of?

CHALLENGES: What obstacles today helped me build confidence in my abilities?

KINDNESS: The self-compassion of today that I will carry into tomorrow.

---

10. Friday

PRESENCE: Sitting with the here & now, the sensations I observe are...

_____
_____
_____

INTENTION: What supports can I use to enter this day with an open heart & mind?

_____
_____
_____

RESOURCES: What growth am I experiencing, & how can I nurture it?

_____
_____
_____
_____

POSITIVES: What am I most grateful for today, & why does it matter to me?

_____
_____
_____

CHALLENGES: How can I end the day feeling positive about the challenges I faced?

_____
_____
_____

KINDNESS: How did I improve my self-talk today, & what can I do to continue?

_____
_____
_____

11. Saturday

PRESENCE: Observing my thoughts without judgement feels like...

INTENTION: One thing I can do to stay calm during stressful moments today is...

RESOURCES: How can I build on the resilience I have shown?

POSITIVES: What is one interaction or conversation that had a positive impact on me today?

CHALLENGES: How did today's challenges make me feel, & why?

KINDNESS: In what ways can I be gentler with myself in moments of frustration?

12. Sunday

PRESENCE: As I scan my body this morning I notice it feels...

INTENTION: What does it look like to forgive myself if things don't go as planned today?

RESOURCES: How can I move forward today with confidence in my abilities?

POSITIVES: What is something I own that I felt grateful to have today?

CHALLENGES: What positive outcomes could come from the challenges today?

KINDNESS: A self-critical thought I had today, & it's replacement in self-compassion.

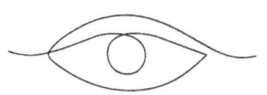

R & R

REFLECT
What obstacles/challenges did you face this week, & how did you handle them?

_____
_____
_____
_____
_____
_____
_____
_____
_____

REFOCUS
How can you build on what you have learned & prepare for potential obstacles/challenges in the week ahead?

_____
_____
_____
_____
_____
_____
_____
_____

13. Monday

PRESENCE: What emotions can I observe, without getting caught up in them?

INTENTION: What would self-acceptance feel & look like as I move through today?

RESOURCES: Today I will observe with curiosity my response to these challenges...

POSITIVES: How did I practice kindness toward myself today?

CHALLENGES: How was I pushed outside my comfort zone, & what did I learn?

KINDNESS: When can I practice more positive self-talk when I feel self-critical?

14. Tuesday

PRESENCE: I can ground myself before beginning the tasks of the day by...

INTENTION: One boundary I can set today to protect my peace...

RESOURCES: A choice I can make today to support balance for my mind &/or body.

POSITIVES: What is one skill or ability I used today that I am thankful for?

CHALLENGES: A setback I faced today that I can turn into a lesson for the future.

KINDNESS: What is one part of myself that I want to embrace with more acceptance?

---

15. Wednesday

PRESENCE: My observations of the sights & sounds surrounding me.

___

___

INTENTION: One small thing I can let go of today that is causing me stress?

___

___

RESOURCES: One way I can acknowledge my strengths today (without needing validation from others)?

___

___

POSITIVES: What did I do today to strengthen a relationship, & how did it feel?

___

___

CHALLENGES: How did I demonstrate flexibility today?

___

___

KINDNESS: I can replace this negative thought today... with this uplifting one tomorrow...

___

___

16. Thursday

PRESENCE: A calm space in my mind feels...

INTENTION: One way I can embrace the flow of the day without rushing through it...

RESOURCES: I can see how far I've come with... and notice these positive side effects...

POSITIVES: Who helped me feel more positive or supported today?

CHALLENGES: How can I improve the way I handle frustration when facing difficulties?

KINDNESS: Tomorrow I can show more emotional care toward myself by...

---

17. Friday

PRESENCE: When I focus fully on each task today without distraction, it will feel...

INTENTION: I will celebrate my uniqueness & individuality today by...

RESOURCES: Balancing my strengths with my calm today looks like...

POSITIVES: Which challenging situation positively impacted my day?

CHALLENGES: What creative solutions did I come up with today?

KINDNESS: I can remind myself of my worth, even when I am deeply challenged by...

18. Saturday

PRESENCE: One feeling or sensation I observe this morning...

_____
_____
_____

INTENTION: Where in my day can I see room to be less hard on myself?

_____
_____
_____

RESOURCES: At these times today... I can remind myself that I have everything I need within me to navigate challenges.

_____
_____
_____

POSITIVES: What is one way in which today's events unfolded that I am thankful for?

_____
_____
_____

CHALLENGES: What did today's difficulty teach me about adapting to change?

_____
_____
_____

KINDNESS: What imperfection did I notice in myself today, & how can I embrace it with love?

_____
_____
_____

19. Sunday

PRESENCE: How it feels to take a deep, mindful breath & pause right now:

___

INTENTION: I can maintain a balance between work & rest today by...

___

RESOURCES: What do I know about myself that will support my tasks & interactions today?

___

POSITIVES: How did I stay focused & productive today, & what made that possible?

___

CHALLENGES: What have I learnt about stepping into discomfort with courage?

___

KINDNESS: What is one thing I can let go of tonight in order to show myself more kindness tomorrow?

___

R & R

REFLECT
What did you learn about yourself this week?

_____
_____
_____
_____
_____
_____
_____
_____

REFOCUS
Plan a way to apply this self-knowledge to improve the week ahead.

_____
_____
_____
_____
_____
_____
_____
_____

20. Monday

PRESENCE: What does it feel like to breathe in this moment & release the need to plan or worry about the day ahead?

_____

_____

_____

INTENTION: What does self-compassion look like for me as I start this day?

_____

_____

RESOURCES: I can remind myself that growth often comes from stepping outside of my comfort zone when...

_____

_____

_____

POSITIVES: Who made me feel valued today, & why am I grateful for it?

_____

_____

_____

CHALLENGES: One positive from today's challenge that I want to remember...

_____

_____

_____

KINDNESS: A self-critical thought I'd like to challenge & replace with a positive one.

_____

_____

_____

21. Tuesday

PRESENCE: What is my mind focusing on at this moment, & how does it affect me?

INTENTION: A kind & compassionate thought I can use for myself today:

RESOURCES: One way I can rely on my inner strength to navigate challenges today.

POSITIVES: What is one thing today that I am truly grateful for?

CHALLENGES: The hardest part of today, & what I learnt about myself from facing it.

KINDNESS: One kind thought I want to tell myself before bed tonight.

---

22. Wednesday

PRESENCE: Listening closely to the signals my body is sending me, I notice...

INTENTION: Where in my day can I offer compassion to myself?

RESOURCES: One area where I'd like to deepen my self-awareness today...

POSITIVES: What positive habit did I follow through with today, & how did it make me feel?

CHALLENGES: What did I gain from the challenges today that I didn't expect?

KINDNESS: What I forgive myself for today (no matter how small).

---

23. Thursday

PRESENCE: I gently check in with my emotions and feel...

INTENTION: When can I remind myself that I am enough, exactly as I am today?

RESOURCES: What is one challenge I can face with strength & self-compassion today?

POSITIVES: What is something about my home that I appreciate today?

CHALLENGES: One small win I experienced today.

KINDNESS: How did I practice self-acceptance today, & what did it feel like?

24. Friday

PRESENCE: The temperature of my breath this morning feels...

INTENTION: I can stay in tune with my emotional needs today by...

RESOURCES: Today, I can focus on aligning with this personal value of mine.

POSITIVES: How did I balance productivity & rest today in a way that felt good?

CHALLENGES: What can I improve on the next time I encounter a challenge like the one I had today?

KINDNESS: An affirming statement I can tell myself to reinforce my self-worth.

---

25. Saturday

PRESENCE: The things I see, hear, feel, touch, taste in the world around me this moment.

INTENTION: I can describe this plan to take a break if I feel overwhelmed today.

RESOURCES: How I can stay true to myself, when faced with opposition or difficulty today:

POSITIVES: Who made my day easier or more enjoyable, & how can I show them gratitude?

CHALLENGES: A flexible solution I found when faced with a challenge.

KINDNESS: I can be more patient with myself when I'm feeling overwhelmed by.

---

26. Sunday

PRESENCE: One thought or concern I can set aside to focus on the present is...

INTENTION: What does it look like to stay present today?

RESOURCES: How can I pace my day productively & avoid feeling rushed?

POSITIVES: How did I respond to a situation today that showed growth in my mindset or behaviour?

CHALLENGES: What have I learnt about staying calm & centred during stressful moments?

KINDNESS: What is one way I can boost my sense of self-worth tomorrow?

R & R

REFLECT
How did your actions this week align with your intentions & priorities for this year?

___

REFOCUS
What steps can you take next week that will continue to direct you towards those intentions and priorities?

___

27. Monday

PRESENCE: Feeling into the soles of my feet this morning, I notice...

_____
_____
_____

INTENTION: One thing I can do to prioritise my well-being today.

_____
_____
_____

RESOURCES: How can I create more peace & harmony in my day?

_____
_____
_____

POSITIVES: Who am I thankful for being in my life today, & why?

_____
_____
_____

CHALLENGES: A creative response I have had to a challenging situation.

_____
_____
_____

KINDNESS: I am learning to be compassionate toward these beautiful flaws & imperfections.

_____
_____
_____

28. Tuesday

PRESENCE: When I feel my mind is wandering, I gently bring it back to the present by...

_____
_____
_____

INTENTION: I can remind myself that I am are worthy of kindness & understanding with these words...

_____
_____
_____

RESOURCES: How can I respond, rather than react, to difficulties today?

_____
_____
_____

POSITIVES: What is one way I made time for self-care today, & how did it enhance my mood?

_____
_____
_____

CHALLENGES: How did I adapt in the day, & what did I learn from adapting?

_____
_____
_____

KINDNESS: I can offer myself more compassion tomorrow by...

_____
_____
_____

29. Wednesday

PRESENCE: When I breathe deeply & consciously I notice...

_____

_____

_____

INTENTION: What would it feel like to go through the day with a peaceful mindset?

_____

_____

_____

RESOURCES: How can I use what I know about myself to improve this day?

_____

_____

_____

POSITIVES: What is one accomplishment from today that I am grateful for?

_____

_____

_____

CHALLENGES: I gained confidence today in... & how I will carry it into the future...

_____

_____

_____

KINDNESS: One affirmation I can repeat to myself tomorrow to encourage positive self-talk.

_____

_____

_____

30. Thursday

PRESENCE: *Focusing on the sound of my breath, I notice...*

___
___
___

INTENTION: *One way I can approach today with ease & self-kindness is...*

___
___
___

RESOURCES: *I can act with both confidence & compassion towards myself & others today when...*

___
___
___

POSITIVES: *What positive feelings am I taking with me into tomorrow?*

___
___
___

CHALLENGES: *Rather than these setbacks today, I can focus on this progress I made...*

___
___
___

KINDNESS: *What is one thing I can forgive myself for today?*

___
___
___

31. Friday

PRESENCE: I gently redirect to the present moment when my mind wanders & notice...

___

INTENTION: How can I create more peace in my day today?

___

RESOURCES: I can remind myself of my strengths when faced with these kinds of difficulties today.

___

POSITIVES: Which person am I thankful for today, & why?

___

CHALLENGES: Which challenge offered me an opportunity for growth today?

___

KINDNESS: How did I take care of my emotional well-being today?

February

Deepening Connection with You

As the summer continues, visualise a moment of stillness & self-reflection. Picture yourself in a peaceful place, perhaps by the beach or in nature, where you feel calm, safe & connected. What are the core values that guide you? See yourself honouring your values in the way you spend your time, make decisions, & care for yourself. Imagine & describe feeling aligned with these & embracing self-compassion as you move through this month.

Belly Breath

To relax the nervous system, reset and activate the vagus nerve (rest and digest state).

1. Find a comfortable place to sit or lie down without disturbance.
2. Place one hand on the chest and one on the belly (abdomen)
3. Inhale through the nose, drawing the breath down toward the belly. With practice, the belly will push out against the hand, while the chest remains still.
4. Hold the breath for a moment at the turning point.
5. Exhale long and gently through the mouth with pursed lips; like you are cooling down hot cuppa. Tighten the tummy muscles and let the belly fall back down. Again, the chest should remain still.
6. Continue for 3-5 minutes, and use this techniques throughout your day to settle nerves and busy mind.

**Please use this technique mindfully & stop if you are feeling strain, overwhelm or find the practice triggering for you.

1. Saturday

PRESENCE: What is my body asking for right now—rest, movement, nourishment, or something else?

_____

_____

_____

INTENTION: Responding to mistakes with patience today, looks like...

_____

_____

_____

RESOURCES: How I want to feel at the end of today, & how I can encourage it?

_____

_____

_____

POSITIVES: What made me smile or laugh today,?

_____

_____

_____

CHALLENGES: How could today's challenge be preparing me for future situations?

_____

_____

_____

KINDNESS: My struggles & imperfections, and the understanding I offer them.

_____

_____

_____

2. Sunday

PRESENCE: Checking in with my emotions, I notice I feel...

_____
_____

INTENTION: What would it look like to accept my emotions today, even the uncomfortable ones?

_____
_____

RESOURCES: I can check on my thoughts & feelings during these situations today...

_____
_____

POSITIVES: What is one piece of good news or positivity that came my way today?

_____
_____

CHALLENGES: How did I stay grounded when dealing with difficulty today?

_____
_____

KINDNESS: Tomorrow I can remind myself that it's okay to be imperfect by...

_____
_____

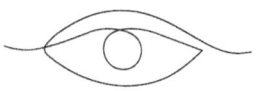

REFLECT
What habits or routines worked well for you this week?

_____
_____
_____
_____
_____
_____
_____
_____

REFOCUS
What new habit or routine can you introduce next week to support your values & intentions?

_____
_____
_____
_____
_____
_____
_____
_____

3. Monday

PRESENCE: When I deepen my breath into my belly, I feel...

_____

_____

INTENTION: I can communicate my needs to others clearly today when...

_____

_____

RESOURCES: I can reflect my values through these actions today.

_____

_____

_____

POSITIVES: What made me feel connected to others today?

_____

_____

CHALLENGES: In a difficult situation I can be compassionate toward myself by...

_____

_____

KINDNESS: The best way I can remind myself that I am enough, just as I am.

_____

_____

_____

4. Tuesday

PRESENCE: One thing I can notice in my environment that I've not paid attention to before...

_____
_____
_____

INTENTION: I can remain grounded in the face of stress today by...

_____
_____
_____

RESOURCES: Some actions I can take today to reflect my strength & resolve are...

_____
_____
_____

POSITIVES: What is something today that reminded me of the goodness in life?

_____
_____
_____

CHALLENGES: What resources did I use today to help me stay strong during challenges?

_____
_____
_____

KINDNESS: When things don't go as planned, I can remind myself of these kind words.

_____
_____
_____

5. Wednesday

PRESENCE: When I close my eyes and release the clutter in my mind it looks...

INTENTION: In which spaces can I remind myself to pause & breathe today?

RESOURCES: I can navigate these priorities today with a sense of ease by...

POSITIVES: One thing that went smoothly or easily for me today.

CHALLENGES: What positive coping mechanisms do I have for stressful challenges?

KINDNESS: What emotion did I allow myself to feel fully today, without judgment?

---

6. Thursday

PRESENCE: Eating breakfast slowly & mindfully feels...

INTENTION: I can nurture my emotions today by...

RESOURCES: In what situations can I use inner calm to anchor my strength today?

POSITIVES: What resource or opportunity was I grateful for today?

CHALLENGES: How have my critical thinking skills helped with a challenge?

KINDNESS: My worth extends beyond my achievements or productivity. I know I have these positive qualities.

7. Friday

PRESENCE: Is there a thought pattern I am noticing that I can choose not to engage with today?

_____

_____

_____

INTENTION: One thing I can do to create balance in my relationships today is...

_____

_____

_____

RESOURCES: In today's potential challenges, I will use this mindful approach.

_____

_____

_____

POSITIVES: What friendship am I grateful for, & why?

_____

_____

_____

CHALLENGES: An experience I've had that has taught me a better version of myself.

_____

_____

_____

KINDNESS: Which area of my life needs more self-compassion practice?

_____

_____

_____

8. Saturday

PRESENCE: The movement of my breath today feels...

INTENTION: What does loving my imperfections look & sound like today?

RESOURCES: When I act in alignment with my values it feels...

POSITIVES: What is one resource or tool that helped me succeed today?

CHALLENGES: When have I trusted myself through a decision or challenge, & how did it feel?

KINDNESS: What can I do tomorrow to continue practicing self-kindness in difficult moments?

---

9. Sunday

PRESENCE: Feeling present and releasing worry about the future feels...

___

INTENTION: One way I can respond to myself with empathy today...

___

RESOURCES: When I trust in myself, decisions today look...

___

POSITIVES: Where did I respond with positivity or strength today?

___

CHALLENGES: What lessons from today can I use to create a better tomorrow?

___

KINDNESS: Where can I put more loving & supportive self-talk into my daily routine?

___

R & R

REFLECT
How did you manage your energy levels throughout the week?

_____
_____
_____
_____
_____
_____
_____
_____
_____

REFOCUS
How can you better balance work, rest, & play in the week ahead?

_____
_____
_____
_____
_____
_____
_____
_____
_____

10. Monday

PRESENCE: When I close my eyes and breathe kindly, I see...

_____
_____
_____

INTENTION: Where/when can I slow down & enjoy the present moment today?

_____
_____
_____

RESOURCES: One challenge I have overcome that proves my ability to grow...

_____
_____
_____

POSITIVES: What opportunity or experience today am I most thankful for?

_____
_____
_____

CHALLENGES: What did today reveal about my strengths or weaknesses?

_____
_____
_____

KINDNESS: One small act of self-kindness I can do for myself tomorrow is...

_____
_____
_____

11. Tuesday

PRESENCE: This morning my energy levels in my body are...

_____

_____

_____

INTENTION: I can remember to speak to myself kindly today when...

_____

_____

_____

RESOURCES: What small step toward growth can I take today, even if it feels uncomfortable?

_____

_____

_____

POSITIVES: What was the most peaceful or calming moment of my day?

_____

_____

_____

CHALLENGES: The challenges & valuable learning experiences I had today...

_____

_____

_____

KINDNESS: When did I show myself compassion, & how did it feel?

_____

_____

_____

12. Wednesday

PRESENCE: What emotions am I noticing this morning?

INTENTION: In what ways can I let go of the need to be perfect today?

RESOURCES: I can check in with my needs & emotions today by...

POSITIVES: What is one strength or skill I used today that I am thankful for?

CHALLENGES: What strategy worked well for me in harder moments today?

KINDNESS: I challenged this negative thought with this positive self-talk replacement.

---

13. Thursday

PRESENCE: When I observe the sensations in my relaxed hands, I notice...

___

INTENTION: One thing I can say "no" to today for my own well-being.

___

RESOURCES: I know myself well enough to know that today I will need this resource.

___

POSITIVES: One thing I learned today that will help me grow in a positive direction.

___

CHALLENGES: One thing I would do differently if I could redo a challenge in my day.

___

KINDNESS: One thing I did today that I completely accept without judgment.

14. Friday

PRESENCE: Right now, in my surroundings I am noticing...

INTENTION: One way I can make things easier for myself today.

RESOURCES: One boundary I can assert in a kind, yet firm, way today.

POSITIVES: What positive memory from today do I want to cherish?

CHALLENGES: I can celebrate the strength I showed at difficult times today by...

KINDNESS: What is one positive affirmation I want to focus on for tomorrow?

---

15. Saturday

PRESENCE: When I still my mind, I find I can let go of this worry easily.

_____

_____

_____

INTENTION: I can notice my reactions today with compassion and soothe myself by...

_____

_____

_____

RESOURCES: I can see myself pause & reflect before reacting to these kinds of difficult situations today.

_____

_____

_____

POSITIVES: One positive decision I made today that I want to continue making.

_____

_____

_____

CHALLENGES: What self-care practices could have helped me during stressful times today?

_____

_____

_____

KINDNESS: How can I show myself more kindness when I'm feeling emotionally vulnerable?

_____

_____

_____

16. Sunday

PRESENCE: When I am fully present for my morning cuppa today, I notice...

_____
_____
_____

INTENTION: One way I can honour my body & its needs today.

_____
_____
_____

RESOURCES: When difficulty shows up today, I will remain peaceful & strong by...

_____
_____
_____

POSITIVES: What is one thing I often take for granted that I felt thankful for today?

_____
_____
_____

CHALLENGES: Today encouraged me to find this new way to approach a problem.

_____
_____
_____

KINDNESS: The positive qualities I see in myself today, & how I can celebrate them.

_____
_____
_____

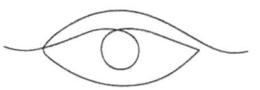

REFLECT
What did you notice about the emotions you had this week?

_____
_____
_____
_____
_____
_____
_____
_____

REFOCUS
How can you carry that emotional awareness into next week?

_____
_____
_____
_____
_____
_____
_____
_____
_____

17. Monday

PRESENCE: When I am patient and curious about my present thoughts, I notice...

___
___
___

INTENTION: When I notice negative self-talk today, I will...

___
___
___

RESOURCES: One way I can be kind to myself today.

___
___
___

POSITIVES: What is one thing I did to protect my energy or maintain balance today?

___
___
___

CHALLENGES: One way I may have grown through a situation/challenge today.

___
___
___

KINDNESS: The mistakes I made today, and why they are okay.

___
___
___

18. Tuesday

PRESENCE: Focusing on my breath, I notice...

INTENTION: Where can I cultivate more harmony in my environment today?

RESOURCES: When I remain calm in the choices I make today, I can feel...

POSITIVES: What positive feedback or recognition did I receive today?

CHALLENGES: These are the successes I choose to remember when I face future difficulties.

KINDNESS: What unrealistic expectation of myself can I lift from my day tomorrow...

---

19. Wednesday

PRESENCE: When I relax my mind and calm my thoughts it feels...

_____
_____
_____

INTENTION: The qualities I have that I will let myself feel guided by today are:

_____
_____
_____

RESOURCES: I can find confidence to approach these tasks today:

_____
_____
_____

POSITIVES: What is one action I want to repeat because of its positive impact?

_____
_____
_____

CHALLENGES: A challenge that passed me today and the learning I will keep from it.

_____
_____
_____

KINDNESS: As I improve how I speak to myself - I hear myself saying...

_____
_____
_____

20. Thursday

PRESENCE: This morning my heart/soul feels...

INTENTION: How I can bring more calm into my interactions today.

RESOURCES: As I am noticing my power, things feel...

POSITIVES: How did I step outside of my comfort zone in a positive way today?

CHALLENGES: What challenge have I overcome that boosted my confidence?

KINDNESS: When I'm feeling overwhelmed, I will offer myself these kind words...

---

21. Friday

PRESENCE: What part of my body feels tense, & what part feels most relaxed?

INTENTION: One way I can show myself understanding today.

RESOURCES: One way I can move myself towards my goals.

POSITIVES: Who supported or helped me today, & how can I show gratitude?

CHALLENGES: One thing I could have done differently to make today easier on me.

KINDNESS: When I'm struggling, I will remind myself...

22. Saturday

PRESENCE: A feeling I am moving through, and how I will gently support myself.

INTENTION: Something I would like to improve on or learn today.

RESOURCES: Where/when can I take my time & respond more thoughtfully today?

POSITIVES: What interaction had a positive affect on my day?

CHALLENGES: Overcoming a challenge makes me feel...

KINDNESS: How did I move away from self-doubt & show myself love today?

---

23. Sunday

PRESENCE: When I slow down & savour the sensations of this moment, it feels...

INTENTION: In what way will I listen & respond to my body's needs today?

RESOURCES: What actions can I take today that align with my values & intentions?

POSITIVES: What am I most grateful for about the timing of events in my day?

CHALLENGES: The mistakes I made & what I learnt from them.

KINDNESS: How I can accept & celebrate my efforts of the day.

R & R

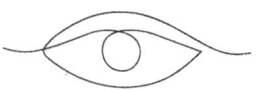

REFLECT
What did you do this week to nurture your relationships with others?

REFOCUS
How can you continue strengthening those connections next week?

24. Monday

PRESENCE: How the space I am in affects my mood, & what I notice about it right now.

___
___
___

INTENTION: One way I can release any tension in my body today?

___
___

RESOURCES: In situations that would typically cause stress today, I remain calm & strong by...

___
___
___

POSITIVES: The positive emotion I experienced the most today, & what created it?

___
___

CHALLENGES: A challenge that taught me about my ability to persevere recently.

___
___

KINDNESS: The kind words that uplifted me today, & where I will use them again.

___
___
___

25. Tuesday

PRESENCE: What is happening around me in this moment now?

INTENTION: One way I can be fully present in my tasks today.

RESOURCES: An area where I can gently push myself out of my comfort zone today.

POSITIVES: What is one thing about my environment today that I felt grateful for?

CHALLENGES: In what ways have I shown I can handle stress better than I thought?

KINDNESS: Tomorrow, I can nurture my emotional needs with compassion by...

---

26. Wednesday

PRESENCE: 5 slow, deep, belly breaths make me feel...

_____
_____

INTENTION: Who will I practice present & open communication with today?

_____
_____

RESOURCES: I will tune into my self-talk during these vulnerable spaces today... & offer these supportive words instead...

_____
_____

POSITIVES: How did I contribute positively to the people/group around me today?

_____
_____

CHALLENGES: An unexpected solution I found during a challenge.

_____
_____

KINDNESS: Did I acknowledge my self-worth today, & how can I ensure I do so tomorrow?

_____
_____

27. Thursday

PRESENCE: The thoughts I am having right now are... without judgement.

INTENTION: I can remind myself that I am doing the best I can today, when...

RESOURCES: It will be useful to stay present & centered when I am facing/doing this today.

POSITIVES: What positive surprise did today bring that I am grateful for?

CHALLENGES: I adapted when this happened today.

KINDNESS: An imperfection/mistake I can reframe with kindness.

28. Friday

PRESENCE: Taking a few moments of stillness to connect with my breath feels...

INTENTION: Today I can maintain a calm & balanced attitude when...

RESOURCES: At these difficult times today... I can focus on this growth it offers me...

POSITIVES: One way I maintained motivation throughout the day.

CHALLENGES: A moment that showed me I am capable of more than I thought.

KINDNESS: What is one thing I can tell myself tonight to ease any worries or self-doubt?

March

Harvest and Gratitude

As autumn begins, visualise a harvest of the seeds you planted earlier in the year. What achievements, habits, or changes have started to take root in your life? See yourself gathering these accomplishments, acknowledging the effort you've put in, & the growth you've witnessed.

Now see, or get a sense of yourself getting closer & closer to... & now <u>at your moment of success</u>. From here, looking back on the steps you take & noticing how it feels to have reached this point.
Look around, what/who do you see? Listen - what does this sound like? What can you feel in mind, body & heart?

Brain Flush

To reduce stress, untangle the mind & give you clarity.

Materials:
- Piece of Paper (loose leaf)
- Pen/pencil
- Timer ready to set for 5-10 minutes
- (Highlighter optional)

A "brain flush" has the intention of moving thoughts, worries, niggles, distractions, to do's & other "mental space blockers" through & out of a busy mind.

1. Set the timer for 5-10 minutes (no less).
2. Start writing!
3. Write without judgement - just let the thoughts settle on the paper.
4. Try not to get bogged down in the details of anything that is upsetting you - make it a dot point to get it out & move on.
5. Write down everything that is on your mind - big worries, small irritations, big to do's & tiny ones, thoughts of the past, the future - write down everything - FLUSH it all out! Write until the timer stops.
6. Optional step - highlight any points of positive action - pop them on your to do list if that feels like it will liberate a thought further.
7. Scrunch, tear, burn or pulp the paper up. Complete the Flush by moving this list on... & away, never to be seen again.

Some prompts if you run dry:
- all of the tasks that you have lingering
- thoughts that are holding you back
- ideas that you're excited about
- worries that are niggling in your mind
- consider mind, body, relationships, home, work, play...
- gratitudes & blessings

**Please use this technique mindfully & stop if you are feeling strain, overwhelm or find the practice triggering for you.

1. Saturday

PRESENCE: Letting the past be passed & focusing on right now, I notice...

___
___
___

INTENTION: At these times, I will choose to be gentle with myself by...

___
___
___

RESOURCES: I will choose self-confidence & self-belief today when...

___
___
___

POSITIVES: One inspiring thing I noticed today.

___
___
___

CHALLENGES: A positive mindset shift I have noticed in myself.

___
___
___

KINDNESS: A kindness I gave to someone today.

___
___
___

2. Sunday

PRESENCE: A thought pattern I am observing myself have.

_____

_____

_____

INTENTION: I can encourage a calm environment in my home/workspace today by...

_____

_____

RESOURCES: I choose to stand confidently in my strengths today when...

_____

_____

_____

POSITIVES: What positive outcome or solution did I find today that made me feel good?

_____

_____

_____

CHALLENGES: A resource or support I have used to handle challenging moments.

_____

_____

KINDNESS: Something I did today that deserves self-praise or acknowledgment?

_____

_____

_____

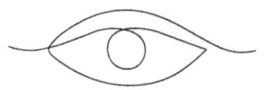

REFLECT
What are you most proud of accomplishing this week?

_____
_____
_____
_____
_____
_____
_____
_____

REFOCUS
What's one goal/intention/value you want to prioritize for next week?

_____
_____
_____
_____
_____
_____
_____
_____

3. Monday

PRESENCE: Staying connected to my body/breath as I move through today will feel...

INTENTION: I can ease up on self-criticism today when...

RESOURCES: To welcome & be open to new opportunities today I will...

POSITIVES: A simple pleasure, (e.g. favorite meal or activity) I am grateful for today.

CHALLENGES: This challenge helped me grow today.

KINDNESS: A moment today where I could treat myself with the same compassion I would offer a friend in a similar situation.

---

4. Tuesday

PRESENCE: Where I am holding emotion in my body right now, & how I can release it gently today?

___
___
___

INTENTION: The strengths & weaknesses I choose to acknowledge & accept today.

___
___
___

RESOURCES: A positive way my actions can affect others today.

___
___
___

POSITIVES: What went better than I expected today?

___
___
___

CHALLENGES: It was at this turning point today that I started to see progress:

___
___
___

KINDNESS: One kind & loving statement I can say to myself after a difficult day:

___
___
___

5. Wednesday

PRESENCE: Feeling into just this present moment, I notice:

___

INTENTION: I will connect back into feeling the present moment during these kinds of stressful/busy times today:

___

RESOURCES: A negative belief or behaviour pattern I can observe & gently question today:

___

POSITIVES: What positive outcome today made me feel supported or cared for?

___

CHALLENGES: A wonderful way to recharge during or at the end of a challenging day.

___

KINDNESS: To nurture more self-acceptance in my thoughts tomorrow I will:

___

6. Thursday

PRESENCE: The sensations I notice in my surroundings—temperature, texture, light:

INTENTION: I can remain calm when I encounter these challenges today:

RESOURCES: Today I can take small and gentle steps towards...

POSITIVES: In what positive way did I handle stress or frustration today?

CHALLENGES: A recent difficulty helped me discover this new strength within myself.

KINDNESS: One negative thought I can let go of tonight... & the positive I replace it with...

7. Friday

PRESENCE: In this quiet moment of stillness, the thought that is challenging me is...

INTENTION: When I observe this thought without attaching to it, it looks....
(colour/texture/temperature)

RESOURCES: I can bring my resilience & power to these situations today.

POSITIVES: A recent challenge that has helped me grow & that I now feel grateful for.

CHALLENGES: What frustrated me the most about today, & how can I approach it differently next time?

KINDNESS: How did I honour my feelings today, & how can I do that more often?

ns
8. Saturday

PRESENCE: Reflecting on the process of something I am doing, rather than the future outcome reminds me...

INTENTION: I can show myself love today by...

RESOURCES: I can plan to cultivate more peace in these aspects of my day today.

POSITIVES: How did I make a positive impact on someone else's day today?

CHALLENGES: A creative solution I have found for a problem that I will use again.

KINDNESS: A kindness I have given to someone that I will give again.

9. Sunday

PRESENCE: When I imagine stepping back & observing my feelings flow this morning, I can describe it as...

_____

_____

INTENTION: At these times my productivity slows... but my worth always stays the same.

_____

_____

RESOURCES: What I can offer myself to feel calm & okay, during moments of frustration?

_____

_____

_____

POSITIVES: What experience today made me feel content or fulfilled?

_____

_____

CHALLENGES: How can I approach tomorrow with a growth mindset?

_____

_____

KINDNESS: I embrace these unique qualities in others, & in myself.

_____

_____

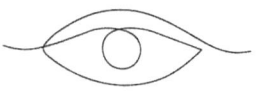

REFLECT
What moment brought you the most joy this week?

_____
_____
_____
_____
_____
_____
_____
_____

REFOCUS
How can you incorporate more joy into your routine next week?

_____
_____
_____
_____
_____
_____
_____
_____

10. Monday

PRESENCE: When I use deep breathing to relax ; my body & mind feel...

INTENTION: My responsibilities today & my intended acts of self-care...

RESOURCES: My instincts are guiding me to....

POSITIVES: Someone I supported or listened to today, & the the gratitude it gives me.

CHALLENGES: An optimistic account of the challenges I have ahead of me.

KINDNESS: A habit or practice I can build that will reinforce positive self-talk in my daily life.

11. Tuesday

PRESENCE: A thought I am curious about.

___

___

___

INTENTION: I can nurture peace in my mind today by...

___

___

___

RESOURCES: A strength I can use to help others today.

___

___

___

POSITIVES: What was the best part of my day, & why did it stand out?

___

___

___

CHALLENGES: The first thought I had when faced with a challenge today, & how it shaped my response.

___

___

___

KINDNESS: A thought & an action from today that offered kindness to myself or others.

___

___

___

12. Wednesday

PRESENCE: Feeling present now feels... I will use this resource at these times/breaks/moments today...

___

___

___

INTENTION: Starting the day without putting unnecessary pressure on myself looks like...

___

___

___

RESOURCES: The actions I will take today to maintain my balance & calm.

___

___

___

POSITIVES: An experience today that opened my heart.

___

___

___

CHALLENGES: A fear or doubt, big or small, that I overcame today.

___

___

___

KINDNESS: Who I have shown compassion towards recently... how it felt... & when I can show myself the same...

___

___

___

13. Thursday

PRESENCE: When I bring attention to my breathing right now, I notice...

___

___

INTENTION: There is room in my day here... to offer myself this same kindness I would to a friend.

___

___

RESOURCES: I have felt confident when... and I can use this feeling to maintain my confidence today when...

___

___

___

POSITIVES: What did I learn today that I am grateful for?

___

___

CHALLENGES: When I am patient with myself during challenging moments I notice...

___

___

KINDNESS: What is one way I can share kindness with others tomorrow?

___

___

14. Friday

PRESENCE: An emotion I am noticing moving through me this morning is...

INTENTION: My worth feels valued when...

RESOURCES: I have noted these triggers... I have for this emotion... and I will soothe/calm myself mindfully through them by...

POSITIVES: A relationship I nurtured in a positive way today.

CHALLENGES: One way I successfully adapted to a situation today.

KINDNESS: One self-judgment I noticed today & the self-acceptance I can offer to replace it.

---

15. Saturday

PRESENCE: What small detail of this morning can I focus on to bring myself into this moment?

_____

_____

_____

INTENTION: One way I can prioritise my mental & emotional health today.

_____

_____

_____

RESOURCES: These priorities I have today... can be supported by these resources I have...

_____

_____

_____

POSITIVES: Something unexpected today that I am thankful for.

_____

_____

_____

CHALLENGES: A challenge that has given me motivation to improve.

_____

_____

_____

KINDNESS: Something kind I said/did for someone today.

_____

_____

_____

16. Sunday

PRESENCE: Being mindful of the natural world around me now, I feel....

INTENTION: When worry comes my way today, I can do this to detach from it & feel ok...

RESOURCES: These personal strengths... will support the decisions I make today.

POSITIVES: One positive outcome of my actions today.

CHALLENGES: A challenge today that I enjoyed and hope more of the same lie ahead.

KINDNESS: In moments of stress or anxiety, I will offer these kind words in self-talk & to those around me.

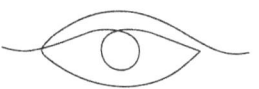

R & R

REFLECT
What was the biggest obstacle you overcame this week?

_____
_____
_____
_____
_____
_____
_____
_____
_____

REFOCUS
What have you learned that will support you to approach future obstacles with confidence?

_____
_____
_____
_____
_____
_____
_____
_____

17. Monday

PRESENCE: I can observe my attention on the now, Pulling it back from future worries or past ruminations feels...

___

INTENTION: A task I can break down into smaller manageable steps today.

___

RESOURCES: In my day ahead, I will show myself compassion when...

___

POSITIVES: What kindness did someone show me today that I appreciate?

___

CHALLENGES: One way I can stay patient & calm when challenges arise.

___

KINDNESS: Someone I would like to check in on more regularly.

___

18. Tuesday

PRESENCE: I have noticed that bringing my attention to the present moment has these greater benefits for me.

_____

_____

INTENTION: An act of self love I can take today.

_____

_____

RESOURCES: Remaining centered in my strength today will allow me to be more open to....

_____

_____

POSITIVES: How did I express or receive love & care today?

_____

_____

CHALLENGES: A problem-solving technique that worked best for me today.

_____

_____

KINDNESS: One thing I want to tell myself tonight to reinforce my sense of worthiness.

_____

_____

19. Wednesday

PRESENCE: When I observe my inner world with curiosity instead of judgment, I notice...

_____

_____

INTENTION: When I make mistakes today, I will offer this kindness to myself...

_____

_____

RESOURCES: An area of my day I will navigate gracefully today.

_____

_____

_____

POSITIVES: One thing about my emotional or mental health that I feel grateful for today.

_____

_____

CHALLENGES: A change I have embraced, even though it felt uncomfortable or difficult at first...

_____

_____

KINDNESS: A flaw I've been hard on myself about, & a softened thought I offer now.

_____

_____

20. Thursday

PRESENCE: Soft breath, deep breath, shallow breath: changing my breath, I notice...

INTENTION: What does a balanced, peaceful day look like for me today?

RESOURCES: What I can bring into my relationships & interactions today.

POSITIVES: A difficulty I am grateful I found the strength/courage to push through today.

CHALLENGES: How I can use that strength to approach tomorrow with more confidence.

KINDNESS: One practice I can use to cultivate more self-kindness in the days ahead.

---

21. Friday

PRESENCE: What does being present in conversations with others today look like & sound like?

_____

_____

_____

INTENTION: A compassionate inner dialogue today starts with these words...

_____

_____

RESOURCES: When self-compassion & self-confidence coexist it feels like...

_____

_____

_____

POSITIVES: What I feel the most thankful for today & how I can express that gratitude.

_____

_____

CHALLENGES: A lesson I have learnt that will help me stay positive in the future.

_____

_____

KINDNESS: Even when it's hard, I can speak kindly to myself, these are my fall back words of kindness...

_____

_____

_____

22. Saturday

PRESENCE: Finding stillness in my mind brings me...

_____

_____

_____

INTENTION: To help me approach challenges calmly & with clarity today, I will...

_____

_____

_____

RESOURCES: I acknowledge these personal strengths as I start my day.

_____

_____

_____

POSITIVES: One small thing that I might normally overlook but feel grateful for.

_____

_____

_____

CHALLENGES: The emotions that came up for me at challenging times today.

_____

_____

_____

KINDNESS: One positive thing I can say to myself right now to show kindness.

_____

_____

23. Sunday

PRESENCE: As I move or stretch my body this morning, the sensations I notice are...

___

___

___

INTENTION: In difficult moments today, I will offer myself compassion by...

___

___

___

RESOURCES: As I challenge myself today by... I will balance in self-care by...

___

___

___

POSITIVES: How did I positively impact someone else's day today?

___

___

___

CHALLENGES: A unique power I have discovered in myself.

___

___

___

KINDNESS: A judgement I chose not to put on myself or someone else today.

___

___

___

R & R

REFLECT
How did you practice self-compassion this week?

_____
_____
_____
_____
_____
_____
_____
_____

REFOCUS
What's one way you can be kinder to yourself next week?

_____
_____
_____
_____
_____
_____
_____
_____

24. Monday

PRESENCE: I notice today, emotionally I am feeling... I can support, move through or prepare for these feelings today by...

___

___

___

INTENTION: When I feel myself comparing myself to others today I will...

___

___

___

RESOURCES: Something unique about me that I will carry confidently into the day.

___

___

___

POSITIVES: One thing about my community that I am grateful for today.

___

___

___

CHALLENGES: My approach to this challenge... showed me I am stronger than I thought.

___

___

___

KINDNESS: How can I support myself (and loved ones) with more love & care during challenging times?

___

___

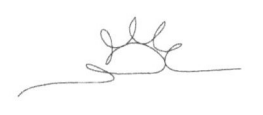

25. Tuesday

PRESENCE: The words I have to describe being present this morning.

___
___
___

INTENTION: Staying within my personal boundaries today looks like...

___
___
___

RESOURCES: A mindful practice I can use today & when it will be useful.

___
___
___

POSITIVES: How I practiced patience or understanding today, & how it affected my interactions.

___
___

CHALLENGES: A mistake I have resolved with flexibility or problem-solving skills.

___
___
___

KINDNESS: A loving act toward myself (or someone else) I can give tomorrow.

___
___
___

26. Wednesday

PRESENCE: When I use my breath to anchor myself in the present moment it helps...

_____

_____

INTENTION: I can avoid rushing through my day & stay balanced by...

_____

_____

RESOURCES: I can visualise myself in ease & flow at this often challenging time of the day.

_____

_____

POSITIVES: Something I relied on today that made my day easier.

_____

_____

CHALLENGES: A time I learnt to be brave in an uncertain situation.

_____

_____

KINDNESS: A mistake I have let go of and the lesson I have kept.

_____

_____

_____

27. Thursday

PRESENCE: My description of a small, often unnoticed detail in my environment.

INTENTION: When I feel my mind starting to overthink... I can tell myself...

RESOURCES: I will use my compassion to support... (someone) through (something) today.

POSITIVES: A small, comforting ritual or routine in my day that I am grateful for.

CHALLENGES: The most empowering part of my day today.

KINDNESS: What encouraging words can I use to support myself tomorrow?

---

28. Friday

PRESENCE: A peaceful moment that quietens the mental noise today feels...

___
___
___

INTENTION: When I start to feel distracted today, I can gently refocus myself by...

___
___
___

RESOURCES: The best way to nurture productivity in my day today will be...

___
___
___

POSITIVES: The joy or creativity I am grateful for today.

___
___
___

CHALLENGES: The positive habits or practices that helped me reduce stress today.

___
___
___

KINDNESS: One thing I can do tomorrow to support my emotional self-care.

___
___
___

29. Saturday

PRESENCE: Breathing mindfully right now feels... & I can use this today when...

___
___
___

INTENTION: I can be kinder to myself when...

___
___
___

RESOURCES: One area of my day where I will try to balance being strong & being gentle with myself.

___
___
___

POSITIVES: Something comforting or reassuring about today that I am grateful for.

___
___
___

CHALLENGES: A moment when I got to practice thinking on my feet.

___
___
___

KINDNESS: Something I can do to make a positive difference to someone else tomorrow.

___
___
___

30. Sunday

PRESENCE: A common story I notice I am telling myself & a way I am rewriting it.

___
___
___

INTENTION: When self-doubt appears today I can release it by...

___
___

RESOURCES: A challenge coming for me today that I will use as a chance to grow...

___
___
___

POSITIVES: Someone or something that made me smile today.

___
___

CHALLENGES: Something I could & something I could not control today.

___
___
___

KINDNESS: When I'm feeling less than perfect, I can show kindness to myself by...

___
___
___

R & R

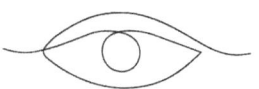

REFLECT
What was the most surprising thing that happened this week, & how did it impact you?

_____
_____
_____
_____
_____
_____
_____
_____

REFOCUS
How can you stay open to unexpected opportunities next week? What kind of opportunities are you seeking?

_____
_____
_____
_____
_____
_____
_____
_____

31. Monday

PRESENCE: Savouring this moment... it looks, feels, sounds, tastes, smells like...

INTENTION: My day ahead in self-acceptance & peace could feel...

RESOURCES: I can make confident, aligned choices today when...

POSITIVES: A positive thought or attitude I want to carry with me into tomorrow.

CHALLENGES: One way I can practice positivity when facing a challenge.

KINDNESS: Did I notice my self-talk improving today, & what can I do to continue?

April

Embracing Change

With the cooler air of autumn settling in, visualise yourself gracefully embracing change. Picture a tree shedding its leaves, releasing what no longer serves it. What can you let go of this month to make space for new opportunities & personal growth? See yourself feeling lighter, more open, & ready for transformation. Imagine yourself navigating change with ease, trusting that each release brings you closer to balance & fulfillment.

Progressive Muscle Relaxation:

To reduce stress, lower heart rate & prepare for calm or sleep.

Lying down, or relaxing in a comfortable chair.

- Begin by focusing on the breath - breathe in slowly, hold the breath, & release slowly... imagine letting tension leave the body as you exhale. Continue this cycle for as long as feels comfortable.

- Starting with the toes, as you breathe in, tighten the feet, curl the toes & the arch, hold & notice the tension there for a cycle of breath (out & in). Breathe out & release the tension in the foot, noticing the new feeling of relaxation.

- Next, focusing on the lower leg. As you breathe in, tense the calf muscles. Hold here noticing the tight sensations for a cycle of breath (out & in). Release the breathe & the tension in the lower legs, notice & hold the feeling of relaxation.

- Now tensing the upper leg & into the hips. Breathe in while squeezing the thighs together & tightening the muscles in the bottom. Hold & notice the tension. Release the breath & soften the upper legs & hips back down, hold that relaxation feeling.

- Breathe in, tense the stomach & chest by pulling the stomach in, tightening the muscles. Hold tension there for a cycle of breath (out & in). Then breathe out & release through the body, noticing the new feeling of relaxation.

- Next, tensing the muscles in the back & shoulders, pull the shoulders together behind you lifting up at the same time. Hold & feel the tension for a cycle of breath (out & in), then release down as you exhale. Notice the difference as it now feels relaxed.

- Breathing in & tensing the full length of the arms. Make a fist & clench all the way up the arms. Hold that tightness for an out & in breath, then exhale & release the tension from the arms down to the fingers, stay here & observe the new relaxation in place.

- Breathe in & move up now into the neck & head, tense the face, the mouth, the eyes & the neck. Hold for a breath cycle (out & in). Exhale & release the tension, notice the softening & the relaxation.

- Now tighten & tense the whole body; from feet to head as you inhale. Hold the tension breathe out, then in. Exhale as the tension releases from the body & you feel that new & wonderfully relaxed feeling through the whole body.

1. Tuesday

PRESENCE: What thoughts are taking up space in my mind, & how can I soften them?

INTENTION: What does a calm & peaceful day look like for me?

RESOURCES: When can I choose to feel strong today?

POSITIVES: A natural beauty or environment around me that I noticed today.

CHALLENGES: A learning experience I had today.

KINDNESS: How can I be more loving toward myself when things are difficult?

---

2. Wednesday

PRESENCE: Tuning in to my body, I notice it needs... today.

___

INTENTION: Some learning I intend to gather through my day today.

___

RESOURCES: How can I be my own best supporter today?

___

POSITIVES: A small, joyful moment I experienced today.

___

CHALLENGES: What future challenges do I look forward to embracing?

___

KINDNESS: My imperfections are perfect for me in this way...

3. Thursday

PRESENCE: Am I noticing any uncomfortable emotions, & can I simply observe them?

INTENTION: If I have any moments of doubt today, I offer this mantra of self-acceptance.

RESOURCES: At these choice points today... I can let my self-awareness inform my decisions & behaviours this way...

POSITIVES: What freedom or choice today am I thankful for?

CHALLENGES: What mindset helped me push through the toughest part of today?

KINDNESS: What is one way I can transform self-criticism into self-encouragement tomorrow?

---

4. Friday

PRESENCE: When can I invite this sense of stillness & mindfulness into my day?

_____

_____

INTENTION: I will respect my own energy levels during these times today.

_____

_____

RESOURCES: Observing my inner dialogue today, I can shift it in this... empowering direction.

_____

_____

_____

POSITIVES: What positive changes have I noticed in myself over this time?

_____

_____

CHALLENGES: What lessons learned from today can I embrace & apply tomorrow?

_____

_____

KINDNESS: How can I be more patient & accepting of my personal journey & growth?

_____

_____

_____

5. Saturday

PRESENCE: Often the space around me reflects the way I feel, so how can I use this knowledge to support myself today?

_____

_____

_____

INTENTION: I can make space for joy & self-acceptance in these ways today.

_____

_____

_____

RESOURCES: I can use both strength & mindfulness to face this challenge... today.

_____

_____

_____

POSITIVES: What made my day feel easier or more manageable?

_____

_____

_____

CHALLENGES: One way I can release any remaining stress from today before I go to bed.

_____

_____

_____

KINDNESS: One way I can make speaking kindly to myself a daily habit.

_____

_____

_____

6. Sunday

PRESENCE: What thoughts are present for me this morning?

___

INTENTION: How could I remain calm in my mind today?

___

RESOURCES: Which of my personal strengths could be my focus today?

___

POSITIVES: What was a moment today that made me feel proud of myself?

___

CHALLENGES: How did I initially respond to the biggest challenge of my day?

___

KINDNESS: What is one kind thing I did for myself today?

REFLECT
What did you learn from a mistake or setback this week?

_____
_____
_____
_____
_____
_____
_____
_____

REFOCUS
Some ways you can turn that lesson into a positive step forward next week:

_____
_____
_____
_____
_____
_____
_____
_____

7. Monday

PRESENCE: What distractions are pulling me away from the present moment right now, & how can I let them go?

_____
_____
_____

INTENTION: In what ways can I practice patience with myself today?

_____
_____
_____

RESOURCES: How can I balance my desire for growth with the need to be kind to myself today?

_____
_____
_____

POSITIVES: What is something I did today that I feel proud & thankful for?

_____
_____
_____

CHALLENGES: What strength did I rely on to get through challenges today?

_____
_____
_____

KINDNESS: How did I take care of my emotional well-being today, & how can I continue to do so?

_____
_____
_____

8. Tuesday

PRESENCE: Which tasks can I approach today with presence & awareness?

INTENTION: I can show myself love & care today when...

RESOURCES: How can I maintain a sense of inner calm today, while also leaning into my strengths?

POSITIVES: How did I feel connected to others in a meaningful way today?

CHALLENGES: A challenge today that allowed me to practice my problem-solving skills.

KINDNESS: What did I do today that made me feel proud of myself?

---

9. Wednesday

PRESENCE: With eyes closed, my mind feels...

_____

_____

INTENTION: Where in my day can I quiet the inner critic & trust myself more?

_____

_____

RESOURCES: How can I respond to challenges today with more awareness & mindfulness?

_____

_____

POSITIVES: What is one thing about my life today that brings me peace or comfort?

_____

_____

CHALLENGES: How were my challenges important to my personal growth?

_____

_____

KINDNESS: How can I show kindness to myself when I make a mistake?

_____

_____

10. Thursday

PRESENCE: Focusing on the rhythm of my breath, how does it feel?

INTENTION: What can I do today to feel more balanced & centred?

RESOURCES: How can I use my self awareness to approach today with more clarity?

POSITIVES: What is one thing I accomplished today, big or small, that I am proud of?

CHALLENGES: What obstacles today helped me build confidence in my abilities?

KINDNESS: The self-compassion of today that I will carry into tomorrow.

---

11. Friday

PRESENCE: Sitting with the here & now, the sensations I observe are...

INTENTION: What supports can I use to enter this day with an open heart & mind?

RESOURCES: What growth am I experiencing, & how can I nurture it?

POSITIVES: What am I most grateful for today, & why does it matter to me?

CHALLENGES: How can I end the day feeling positive about the challenges I faced?

KINDNESS: How did I improve my self-talk today, & what can I do to keep progressing?

---

12. Saturday

PRESENCE: Observing my thoughts without judgement feels like...

INTENTION: One thing I can do to stay calm during stressful moments today is...

RESOURCES: How can I build on the resilience I have shown?

POSITIVES: What is one interaction or conversation that had a positive impact on me today?

CHALLENGES: How did today's challenges make me feel, & why?

KINDNESS: In what ways can I be gentler with myself in moments of frustration?

---

13. Sunday

PRESENCE: As I scan my body this morning I notice it feels...

INTENTION: What does it look like to forgive myself today, if things don't go as planned?

RESOURCES: How can I move forward today with confidence in my abilities?

POSITIVES: What is something I own that I felt grateful to have today?

CHALLENGES: What positive outcomes could come from the challenges today?

KINDNESS: A self-critical thought I had today, & it's replacement in self-compassion.

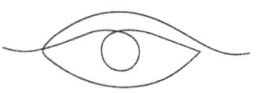

REFLECT
What small wins did you achieve this week that you might otherwise let be overlooked?

_____
_____
_____
_____
_____
_____
_____
_____

REFOCUS
How can you acknowledge & celebrate small wins next week?

_____
_____
_____
_____
_____
_____
_____
_____

14. Monday

PRESENCE: What emotions can I observe, without getting caught up in them?

INTENTION: What would self-acceptance feel like as I move through today?

RESOURCES: Today I will observe with curiosity my response to these challenges...

POSITIVES: How did I practice kindness toward myself today?

CHALLENGES: How was I pushed outside my comfort zone, & what did I learn?

KINDNESS: I can practice more positive self-talk when I feel self-critical in these times of my day.

---

15. Tuesday

PRESENCE: I can ground myself before beginning the tasks of the day by...

INTENTION: One boundary I can set today to protect my peace is...

RESOURCES: A choice I can make today to support balance for my mind &/or body,

---

POSITIVES: What is one skill or ability I used today that I am thankful for?

CHALLENGES: A setback I faced today that I can turn into a lesson for the future.

KINDNESS: What is one part of myself that I want to embrace with more acceptance?

---

16. Wednesday

PRESENCE: My observations of the sights & sounds surrounding me.

___
___
___

INTENTION: One small thing I can let go of today that is causing me stress?

___
___

RESOURCES: One way I can acknowledge my strengths today (without needing validation from others)?

___
___
___

POSITIVES: What did I do today to strengthen a relationship, & how did it feel?

___
___

CHALLENGES: How did I demonstrate flexibility today?

___
___

KINDNESS: I can replace this negative thought... with this uplifting one... tomorrow.

___
___
___

17. Thursday

PRESENCE: *A calm space in my mind feels like...*

_____

_____

INTENTION: *One way I can embrace the flow of the day without rushing through it...*

_____

_____

RESOURCES: *I can enjoy growth today without pushing myself too hard by...*

_____

_____

POSITIVES: *Who helped me feel more positive or supported today?*

_____

_____

CHALLENGES: *How can I improve the way I handle frustration when facing difficulties?*

_____

_____

KINDNESS: *Tomorrow I can show more emotional care toward myself by...*

_____

_____

18. Friday

PRESENCE: Focusing fully on each task without distraction today will feel...

INTENTION: I will celebrate my uniqueness & individuality today by...

RESOURCES: Balancing my strength & inner peace today looks like...

POSITIVES: Which challenging situation positively impacted my day?

CHALLENGES: What creative solutions did I come up with today?

KINDNESS: I can remind myself of my worth, even when I am deeply challenged by...

19. Saturday

PRESENCE: One inner feeling or sensation I observe this morning.

___

INTENTION: Where in my day can I see room to be less hard on myself?

___

RESOURCES: At these times today... I can remind myself that I have everything I need within me to navigate challenges.

___

POSITIVES: What is one way in which today's events unfolded that I am thankful for?

___

CHALLENGES: What did today's difficulty teach me about adapting to change?

___

KINDNESS: What imperfection did I notice in myself today, & how can I embrace it with love?

___

20. Sunday

PRESENCE: How it feels to take a deep, mindful breath & pause right now.

INTENTION: I can maintain a balance between work & rest today by...

RESOURCES: What do I know about myself that will support my tasks & interactions today?

POSITIVES: How did I stay focused & productive today, & what made that possible?

CHALLENGES: What have I learnt about stepping into discomfort with courage?

KINDNESS: What is one thing I can let go of tonight in order to show myself more kindness tomorrow?

REFLECT
What decision did you make this week that you feel proud of?

_____
_____
_____
_____
_____
_____
_____
_____

REFOCUS
Are there decisions to be made next week that you can align with your values?

_____
_____
_____
_____
_____
_____
_____
_____

21. Monday

PRESENCE: What does it feel like to breathe in this moment & release the need to plan or worry about the rest of the day?

_____
_____
_____

INTENTION: What does self-compassion look like for me as I start this day?

_____
_____
_____

RESOURCES: I can remind myself that growth often comes from stepping outside of my comfort zone when...

_____
_____
_____

POSITIVES: Who made me feel valued today, & why am I grateful for it?

_____
_____
_____

CHALLENGES: One positive from today's challenge that I want to remember.

_____
_____
_____

KINDNESS: A self-critical thought I'd like to challenge & replace with this positive one.

_____
_____
_____

22. Tuesday

PRESENCE: What is my mind focusing on at this moment, & how does it affect me?

___

___

INTENTION: A kind & compassionate thought I can use for myself today.

___

___

RESOURCES: One way I can rely on my inner strength to navigate challenges today:

___

___

POSITIVES: What is one thing today that I am truly grateful for?

___

___

CHALLENGES: The hardest part of today, & what I learnt about myself from facing it.

___

___

KINDNESS: One kind thought I want to tell myself before bed tonight.

___

___

23. Wednesday

PRESENCE: Listening closely to the signals my body is sending me, I notice...

INTENTION: Where in my day can I offer compassion to myself?

RESOURCES: One area where I'd like to deepen my self-awareness today...

POSITIVES: What positive habit did I follow through with today, & how did it make me feel?

CHALLENGES: What did I gain from the challenges today that I didn't expect?

KINDNESS: What I forgive myself for today (no matter how small).

---

24. Thursday

PRESENCE: I gently check in with my emotions and feel...

INTENTION: When can I remind myself that I am enough, exactly as I am today?

RESOURCES: What is one challenge I can face with strength & self-compassion today?

POSITIVES: What is something about my home that I appreciate today?

CHALLENGES: One small win I experienced today.

KINDNESS: How did I practice self-acceptance today, & what did it feel like?

---

25. Friday

PRESENCE: The temperature of my breath this morning feels...

_____
_____
_____

INTENTION: I can stay in tune with my emotional needs today by...

_____
_____
_____

RESOURCES: Today I can focus on aligning with this personal value of mine.

_____
_____
_____

POSITIVES: How did I balance productivity & rest today in a way that felt good?

_____
_____
_____

CHALLENGES: What can I improve on the next time I encounter a challenge like the one I had today?

_____
_____
_____

KINDNESS: An affirming statement I can tell myself to reinforce my feelings of self-worth.

_____
_____
_____

26. Saturday

PRESENCE: The things I see, hear, feel, touch, taste in the world around me this day.

_____

_____

_____

INTENTION: I describe this plan to take a break if I feel overwhelmed today.

_____

_____

RESOURCES: How I can stay true to myself, when faced with opposition or difficulty today.

_____

_____

_____

POSITIVES: Who made my day easier or more enjoyable, & how can I show them gratitude?

_____

_____

CHALLENGES: How can I build on the flexibility I have shown when faced with a challenge?

_____

_____

KINDNESS: I can be more patient with myself when I'm feeling overwhelmed by...

_____

_____

27. Sunday

PRESENCE: One thought or concern I can set aside to focus on the present is...

INTENTION: What does it look like to stay present today?

RESOURCES: How can I pace my day productively & avoid feeling rushed?

POSITIVES: How did I respond to a situation today that showed growth in my mindset or behaviour?

CHALLENGES: What have I learnt about staying calm & centred during stressful moments?

KINDNESS: What is one way I can boost my sense of self-worth tomorrow?

R & R

REFLECT
How did you handle moments of stress or overwhelm this week?

_____
_____
_____
_____
_____
_____
_____
_____

REFOCUS
The techniques or strategies you can use next week to manage stress more effectively:

_____
_____
_____
_____
_____
_____
_____
_____
_____

28. Monday

PRESENCE: Feeling into the soles of my feet this morning, I notice...

INTENTION: One thing I can do to prioritise my well-being today.

RESOURCES: How can I use my strength to create more peace & harmony in my day?

POSITIVES: Who am I thankful for being in my life today, & why?

CHALLENGES: A creative response I have had to a challenging situation.

KINDNESS: I am learning to be compassionate toward these beautiful flaws & imperfections.

29. Tuesday

PRESENCE: When I feel my mind is wandering, I gently bring it back to the present by...

INTENTION: I can remind myself that I am are worthy of kindness & understanding with these words...

RESOURCES: How can I respond, rather than react, to difficulties today?

POSITIVES: What is one way I made time for self-care today, & how did it enhance my mood?

CHALLENGES: How did I adapt in the day, & what did I learn from adapting?

KINDNESS: I can offer myself more compassion tomorrow by...

---

30. Wednesday

PRESENCE: When I breathe deeply & consciously I notice...

INTENTION: How can I create more peace in my day today?

RESOURCES: How can I use what I know of my self to improve this day?

POSITIVES: What is one accomplishment from today that I am grateful for?

CHALLENGES: The confidence I gained today, & how I will carry it into future challenges?

KINDNESS: One affirmation I can repeat to myself tomorrow to encourage positive self-talk.

Cultivating Inner Warmth

As the days grow shorter & winter approaches, visualise yourself wrapping yourself in warmth & comfort. Picture a glowing fire inside you that represents your inner strength & resilience. What practices help you maintain this warmth, even as the external world cools? See yourself focusing on self-care, personal reflection, & building emotional resilience. Imagine that this inner warmth sustains you throughout the month, allowing you to feel grounded & centred. Reflect on this inner glow from you. What keeps it burning? What does it fuel? What does the warm glow of light illuminate for you?

More Words for You

Highlight the affirmations that feel right for you, or close your eyes and let your finger land on one to use today!

Personal Empowerment:

- I am the author of my own story.
- I take responsibility for my happiness & success.
- I am worthy of achieving my dreams.
- I radiate confidence & positivity.
- I am a powerful force for positive change in my life.
- I embrace my personal power & create the life I want.
- I take control of my happiness & make decisions that are right for me.
- I am in control of my destiny & my choices shape my future.
- I have the power to manifest my dreams.

Balance & Well-Being:

- I honor my body by taking care of it.
- I make time for the things that nourish my soul.
- My mental & emotional health are priorities.
- I take time to nurture myself.
- I am deserving of rest & relaxation.
- I embrace balance in all areas of my life.
- I honor my emotions & trust they will pass.
- I choose to focus on what I can control & release the rest.
- My well-being is my top priority.

Resilience & Perseverance:

- I am resilient, strong, & brave.
- No matter what comes my way, I will overcome it.
- I am capable of achieving greatness.
- I trust myself to navigate life's challenges.
- I grow stronger with every challenge I face.
- My strength is greater than any struggle.
- I am determined, persistent, & successful.
- I am learning to trust the process.
- I choose to focus on the positives in every situation.

Empowerment in Relationships:

- I communicate my needs & feelings with ease.
- I surround myself with people who respect & love me.
- I attract positive & supportive people into my life.
- I choose relationships that nurture my well-being.
- I respect & honor my boundaries.
- I deserve to be treated with love & respect.
- I release relationships that no longer serve my highest good.
- I am worthy of deep, fulfilling love.

1. Thursday

PRESENCE: Focusing on the sound of my breath, I notice...

_____
_____
_____

INTENTION: One way I can approach today with ease & self-kindness is...

_____
_____
_____

RESOURCES: I can act with both confidence & compassion towards myself & others today when...

_____
_____
_____

POSITIVES: What positive feelings am I taking with me into tomorrow?

_____
_____
_____

CHALLENGES: Rather than these setbacks, I can focus on this progress I made today.

_____
_____
_____

KINDNESS: What is one thing I can forgive myself for today?

_____
_____
_____

2. Friday

PRESENCE: I gently redirect to the present moment when my mind wanders & notice...

_____

_____

_____

INTENTION: What would it feel like to go through the day with a peaceful mindset?

_____

_____

_____

RESOURCES: I can remind myself of my strengths when faced with these kinds of difficulties today.

_____

_____

_____

POSITIVES: Which person am I thankful for today, & why?

_____

_____

_____

CHALLENGES: Which challenge offered me an opportunity for growth today?

_____

_____

_____

KINDNESS: How did I take care of my emotional well-being today?

_____

_____

_____

3. Saturday

PRESENCE: What is my body asking for right now—rest, movement, nourishment, or something else?

_____

_____

_____

INTENTION: Responding to mistakes with patience today, looks like...

_____

_____

_____

RESOURCES: How I want to feel at the end of today, & how I can encourage it?

_____

_____

_____

POSITIVES: What made me smile or laugh today,?

_____

_____

_____

CHALLENGES: How could today's challenge be preparing me for future situations?

_____

_____

_____

KINDNESS: My struggles & imperfections, and the understanding I offer them.

_____

_____

_____

4. Sunday

PRESENCE: Checking in with my emotions, I notice I feel...

_____

_____

_____

INTENTION: What would it look like to accept my emotions today, even the uncomfortable ones?

_____

_____

_____

RESOURCES: I can check on my thoughts & feelings during these situations today...

_____

_____

_____

POSITIVES: What is one piece of good news or positivity that came my way today?

_____

_____

_____

CHALLENGES: How did I stay grounded when dealing with difficulty today?

_____

_____

_____

KINDNESS: Tomorrow I can remind myself that it's okay to be imperfect by...

_____

_____

_____

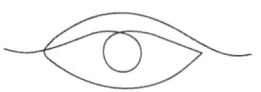

REFLECT
What moment of growth did you experience this week, even if it was difficult?

_____
_____
_____
_____
_____
_____
_____
_____
_____

REFOCUS
How can you continue building on that growth in the coming week?

_____
_____
_____
_____
_____
_____
_____
_____
_____

5. Monday

PRESENCE: When I deepen my breath into my belly, I feel...

___

___

___

INTENTION: I can communicate my needs to others clearly today when...

___

___

___

RESOURCES: I can reflect my values through these actions today.

___

___

___

POSITIVES: What made me feel connected to others today?

___

___

___

CHALLENGES: In a difficult situation I can be compassionate toward myself by...

___

___

___

KINDNESS: The best way I can remind myself that I am enough, just as I am.

___

___

___

6. Tuesday

PRESENCE: One thing I can notice in my environment that I've not paid attention to before.

INTENTION: I can remain grounded in the face of stress today by...

RESOURCES: Some actions I can take today to reflect my strength & resolve.

POSITIVES: What is something today that reminded me of the goodness in life?

CHALLENGES: What resources did I use today to help me stay strong during challenges?

KINDNESS: When things don't go as planned, I can remind myself of these kind words.

---

7. Wednesday

PRESENCE: When I close my eyes & release the clutter in my mind it looks...

_____

_____

_____

INTENTION: In which spaces can I remind myself to pause & breathe today?

_____

_____

RESOURCES: I can navigate the priorites today with a sense of ease by...

_____

_____

_____

POSITIVES: One thing that went smoothly or easily for me today.

_____

_____

CHALLENGES: What positive coping mechanisms do I have for stressful challenges?

_____

_____

_____

KINDNESS: What emotion did I allow myself to feel fully today, without judgment?

_____

_____

_____

8. Thursday

PRESENCE: While eating breakfast slowly & mindfully, I notice...

___

INTENTION: I can nurture my emotions today by...

___

RESOURCES: In what situations can I use inner calm to anchor my strength today?

___

POSITIVES: What resource or opportunity was I grateful for today?

___

CHALLENGES: How have my critical thinking skills helped with a challenge?

___

KINDNESS: My worth extends beyond my achievements or productivity. I know I have these positive qualities.

___

9. Friday

PRESENCE: Is there a thought pattern I am noticing that I can choose not to engage with today?

___

___

___

INTENTION: One thing I can do to create balance in my relationships today is...

___

___

___

RESOURCES: In today's potential challenges, I will use this mindful approach.

___

___

___

POSITIVES: What friendship am I grateful for, & why?

___

___

___

CHALLENGES: An experience I've had that has taught me a better version of myself.

___

___

___

KINDNESS: Which area of my life needs more self-compassion practice?

___

___

___

10. Saturday

PRESENCE: The movement of my breath today feels...

INTENTION: What does loving my imperfections look sound like today?

RESOURCES: When I act in alignment with my values it feels...

POSITIVES: What is one resource or tool that helped me succeed today?

CHALLENGES: When have I trusted myself through a decision or challenge, & how did it feel?

KINDNESS: What can I do tomorrow to continue practicing self-kindness in difficult moments?

---

11. Sunday

PRESENCE: Feeling present and releasing worry about the future feels...

_____
_____
_____

INTENTION: One way I can respond to myself with empathy today...

_____
_____
_____

RESOURCES: When I trust in myself, decisions today look...

_____
_____
_____

POSITIVES: Where did I respond with positivity or strength today?

_____
_____
_____

CHALLENGES: What lessons from today can I use to create a better tomorrow?

_____
_____
_____

KINDNESS: Where can I put more loving & supportive self-talk into my daily routine?

_____
_____
_____

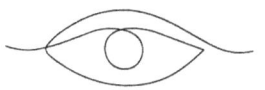

R & R

REFLECT
What positive feedback or support did you receive this week, & how did it make you feel?

_____
_____
_____
_____
_____
_____
_____
_____
_____

REFOCUS
How can you use this feedback to improve or inspire your actions next week?

_____
_____
_____
_____
_____
_____
_____
_____
_____

12. Monday

PRESENCE: When I close my eyes and breathe kindly, I see...

_____

_____

INTENTION: Where/when can I slow down & enjoy the present moment today?

_____

_____

RESOURCES: One challenge I have overcome that proves my ability to grow is...

_____

_____

_____

POSITIVES: What opportunity or experience today am I most thankful for?

_____

_____

_____

CHALLENGES: What did today reveal about my strengths or weaknesses?

_____

_____

_____

KINDNESS: One small act of self-kindness I can do for myself tomorrow.

_____

_____

_____

13. Tuesday

PRESENCE: This morning my energy levels in my body are...

INTENTION: I can remember to speak to myself kindly today when...

RESOURCES: What small step toward growth can I take today, even if it feels uncomfortable?

POSITIVES: What was the most peaceful or calming moment of my day?

CHALLENGES: The challenges & valuable learning experiences I had today...

KINDNESS: When did I show myself compassion, & how did it feel?

---

14. Wednesday

PRESENCE: What emotions am I noticing this morning?

_____

_____

INTENTION: In what ways can I let go of the need to be perfect today?

_____

_____

RESOURCES: I can check in with my needs & emotions today by...

_____

_____

_____

POSITIVES: What is one strength or skill I used today that I am thankful for?

_____

_____

CHALLENGES: What strategy worked well for me in harder moments today?

_____

_____

KINDNESS: I challenged this negative thought with this positive self-talk replacement.

_____

_____

_____

15. Thursday

PRESENCE: When I observe the sensations in my relaxed hands, I notice...

INTENTION: One thing I can say "no" to today for my own well-being.

RESOURCES: I know myself well enough to know that today I will need this resource.

POSITIVES: One thing I learned today that will help me grow in a positive direction.

CHALLENGES: One thing I would do differently if I could redo a challenge in my day.

KINDNESS: One thing I did today that I completely accept without judgment.

---

16. Friday

PRESENCE: Right now, in my surroundings I am noticing...

INTENTION: One way I can make things easier for myself today.

RESOURCES: One boundary I can assert in a kind, yet firm, way today.

POSITIVES: What positive memory from today do I want to cherish?

CHALLENGES: I can celebrate the strength I showed at difficult times today by...

KINDNESS: How can I show myself more kindness when I'm feeling emotionally vulnerable?

---

17. Saturday

PRESENCE: When I still my mind, I find I can let go of this worry easily.

___

INTENTION: I can notice my reactions today with compassion and soothe myself by...

___

RESOURCES: I can see myself pause & reflect before reacting to these kinds of difficult situations today.

___

POSITIVES: One positive decision I made today that I want to continue making.

___

CHALLENGES: What self-care practices could have helped me during stressful times today?

___

KINDNESS: What is one positive affirmation I want to focus on for tomorrow?

___

18. Sunday

PRESENCE: When I am fully present for my morning cuppa today, I notice...

INTENTION: One way I can honour my body & its needs today.

RESOURCES: When difficulty shows up today, I will remain peaceful & strong by...

POSITIVES: What is one thing I often take for granted that I felt thankful for today?

CHALLENGES: Today encouraged me to find this new way to approach a problem.

KINDNESS: The positive qualities I see in myself today, & how I can celebrate them.

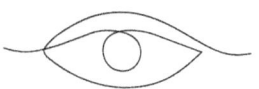

REFLECT
What did you let go of this week that no longer served you?

_____
_____
_____
_____
_____
_____
_____
_____

REFOCUS
How can you create more space for positive change in the upcoming week?

_____
_____
_____
_____
_____
_____
_____
_____

19. Monday

PRESENCE: When I am patient and curious about my present thoughts, I notice...

_____

_____

INTENTION: When I notice negative self-talk today, I will...

_____

_____

RESOURCES: One way I can be kind to myself today.

_____

_____

POSITIVES: What is one thing I did to protect my energy or maintain balance today?

_____

_____

CHALLENGES: One way I may have grown through a situation/challenge today.

_____

_____

KINDNESS: The mistakes I made today, & why they are okay.

_____

_____

20. Tuesday

PRESENCE: Focusing on my breath, I notice...

INTENTION: Where can I cultivate more harmony in my environment today?

RESOURCES: When I remain calm in the choices I make today, I feel...

POSITIVES: What positive feedback or recognition did I receive today?

CHALLENGES: These successes I choose to remember when I face future difficulties.

KINDNESS: What unrealistic expectation of myself can I lift from my day tomorrow.

---

21. Wednesday

PRESENCE: When I relax my mind & calm my thoughts it feels...

_____
_____
_____

INTENTION: The qualities I have, that I will let myself feel guided by today are...

_____
_____
_____

RESOURCES: I can find confidence to approach these tasks today.

_____
_____
_____

POSITIVES: What is one action I want to repeat because of its positive impact?

_____
_____
_____

CHALLENGES: A challenge that passed me today & the learning I will keep from it.

_____
_____
_____

KINDNESS: As I improve how I speak to myself - I hear myself saying...

_____
_____
_____

22. Thursday

PRESENCE: This morning my heart/soul feels...

INTENTION: I can bring more calm into these... interactions today.

RESOURCES: As I am noticing my power, things feel...

POSITIVES: How did I step outside of my comfort zone in a positive way today?

CHALLENGES: What challenge have I overcome that boosted my confidence?

KINDNESS: When I'm feeling overwhelmed, I will offer myself these kind words.

23. Friday

PRESENCE: What part of my body feels the most relaxed, & what part feels tense?

___

___

___

INTENTION: One way I can show myself understanding today.

___

___

___

RESOURCES: One way I can challenge myself today towards my goals.

___

___

___

POSITIVES: Who supported or helped me today, & how can I show gratitude?

___

___

___

CHALLENGES: One thing I could have done differently to make today easier on me

___

___

___

KINDNESS: When I'm struggling, I will remind myself...

___

___

___

24. Saturday

PRESENCE: A feeling I am moving through, & how I will gently support myself.

INTENTION: Something I would like to improve on or learn today.

RESOURCES: Where/when can I take my time & respond more thoughtfully today?

POSITIVES: What interaction had a positive affect on my day?

CHALLENGES: Overcoming a challenge makes me feel...

KINDNESS: How did I move away from self-doubt & show myself love today?

---

25. Sunday

PRESENCE: When I slow down & savour the sensations of this moment, it feels...

INTENTION: In what way will I listen and respond to my body's needs today?

RESOURCES: What actions can I take today that align with my values & intentions?

POSITIVES: What am I most grateful for about the timing of events in my day?

CHALLENGES: The mistakes I made & what I learnt from them.

KINDNESS: How I can accept & celebrate my efforts of the day.

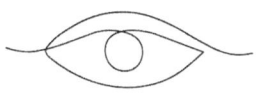

REFLECT
*What progress did you make toward a goal this week?
(personal or professional)*

___

REFOCUS
What's the next step you can take in the week ahead to move closer to that goal?

___

26. Monday

PRESENCE: How the space I am in affects my mood, & what I notice about it right now.

___

___

INTENTION: One way I can release any tension in my body today.

___

___

RESOURCES: In situations that would typically cause stress today, I remain calm & strong by...

___

___

___

POSITIVES: The positive emotion I experienced the most today, & what created it?

___

___

CHALLENGES: A challenge that taught me about my ability to persevere recently was.

___

___

KINDNESS: The kind words that uplifted me today, & where I will use them again.

___

___

27. Tuesday

PRESENCE: What is happening around me in this moment now?

_____

_____

INTENTION: One way I can be fully present in my tasks today.

_____

_____

RESOURCES: An area where I can gently push myself out of my comfort zone today.

_____

_____

POSITIVES: What is one thing about my environment today that I felt grateful for?

_____

_____

CHALLENGES: In what ways have I shown I can handle stress better than I thought?

_____

_____

KINDNESS: Tomorrow, I can nurture my emotional needs with compassion by...

_____

_____

28. Wednesday

PRESENCE: 5 slow, deep, belly breaths make me feel...

_____
_____

INTENTION: Who will I practice present & open communication with today?

_____
_____

RESOURCES: I will tune into my self-talk during these... vulnerable spaces today, & offer these... supportive words instead.

_____
_____
_____

POSITIVES: How did I contribute positively to the people/group around me today?

_____
_____

CHALLENGES: An unexpected solution I found during a challenge.

_____
_____

KINDNESS: Did I acknowledge my self-worth today, & how can I ensure I do so tomorrow?

_____
_____
_____

29. Thursday

PRESENCE: The thoughts I am having right now are... without judgement.

___
___
___

INTENTION: I can remind myself that I am doing the best I can today, when...

___
___
___

RESOURCES: It will be useful to stay present & centered when I am facing/doing this today.

___
___
___

POSITIVES: What positive surprise did today bring that I am grateful for?

___
___
___

CHALLENGES: I adapted when this happened today.

___
___
___

KINDNESS: An imperfection/mistake I can reframe with kindness.

___
___
___

30. Friday

PRESENCE: Taking a few moments of stillness to connect with my breath feels...

___

___

___

INTENTION: Today I can maintain a calm & balanced attitude when...

___

___

___

RESOURCES: At these difficult times today, I can focus on this growth it offers me.

___

___

___

___

POSITIVES: One way I maintained motivation throughout the day...

___

___

___

___

CHALLENGES: A moment that showed me I am capable of more than I thought...

___

___

___

KINDNESS: What is one thing I can tell myself tonight to ease any worries or self-doubt?

___

___

___

31. Saturday

PRESENCE: Letting the past be passed & focusing on right now, I notice...

_____
_____
_____

INTENTION: At these times, I will choose to be gentle with myself by...

_____
_____
_____

RESOURCES: I will choose self-confidence & self-belief today when...

_____
_____
_____

POSITIVES: One inspiring thing I noticed today.

_____
_____
_____

CHALLENGES: A positive mindset shift I have noticed in myself.

_____
_____

KINDNESS: A kindness I gave to someone today.

_____
_____
_____

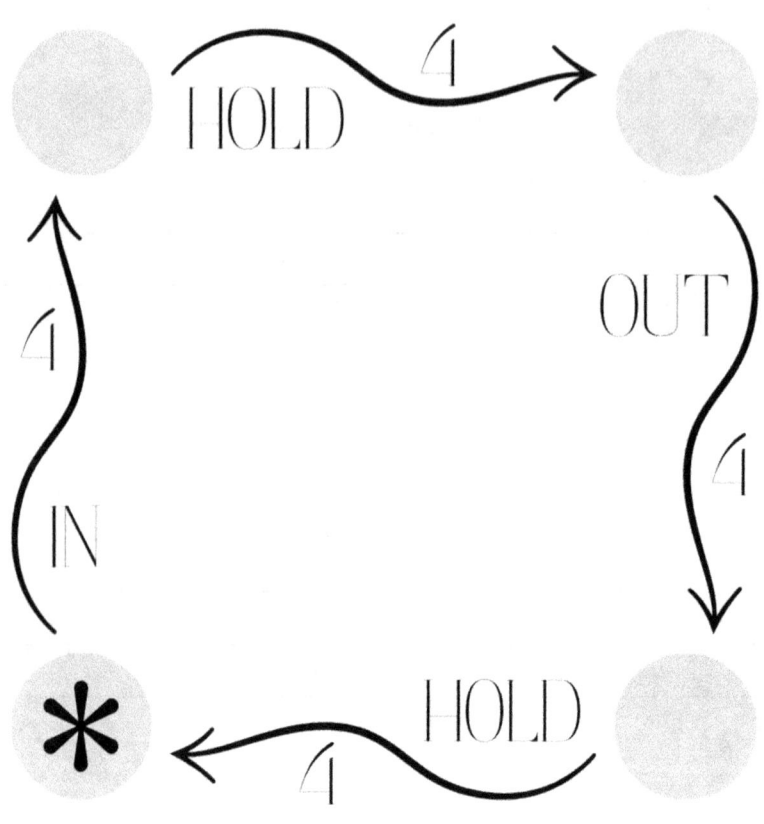

Box Breathing:

To clear the mind, and create a sense of calm and readiness

Trace the arrows with your pointer finger, starting at the ✱.
Change direction at the dots.
Breathe in for the count of 4.
Hold for the count of 4.
Exhale for a count of 4.
Hold for a count of 4.
Continue for 1 minute, build up to 3 minutes.

**Please use this technique mindfully & stop if you are feeling strain, overwhelm or find the practice triggering for you.

Rest & Rejuvenation

Winter brings it's own opportunities for growth, resilience & renewal. Visualise yourself amongst the smaller things that bring you joy during the colder months. Picture yourself in the comfort of a warm drink, a good book, or a moment spent wrapped up and watching the rain outside. Imagine embracing these small slow moments, finding warmth & joy in each one. Imagine settling in to the full recharge available as the world quietens outside and you find the quiet within. What opportunities to rest and rejuvenate do you see presented, and what resources do you feel yourself stockpiling for when the ice melts...

1. Sunday

PRESENCE: A thought pattern I am observing myself have.

_____

_____

_____

INTENTION: I can encourage a calm environment in my home/workspace today by...

_____

_____

_____

RESOURCES: I choose to stand confidently in my strengths today when...

_____

_____

_____

POSITIVES: What positive outcome or solution did I find today that made me feel good?

_____

_____

_____

CHALLENGES: A resource or support I use to handle challenging moments.

_____

_____

_____

KINDNESS: Something I did today that deserves self-praise or acknowledgment.

_____

_____

_____

R & R

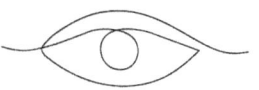

REFLECT
How did you maintain your focus & motivation this week?

_____
_____
_____
_____
_____
_____
_____
_____

REFOCUS
What can you do next week to keep your motivation strong?

_____
_____
_____
_____
_____
_____
_____
_____

2. Monday

PRESENCE: Staying connected to my body as I move through today will feel...

INTENTION: I can ease up on self-criticism today when...

RESOURCES: To welcome & be open to new opportunities today I will...

POSITIVES: A simple pleasure, (e.g. favorite meal or activity) I am grateful for today.

CHALLENGES: This challenge helped me grow today.

KINDNESS: A moment today where I could treat myself with the same compassion I would offer a friend in a similar situation.

---

3. Tuesday

PRESENCE: Where I am holding emotion in my body right now, & how can I release it gently today?

_____

_____

_____

INTENTION: The strengths & weaknesses I choose to acknowledge & accept today.

_____

_____

_____

RESOURCES: A positive way my actions can affect others today.

_____

_____

_____

POSITIVES: What went better than I expected today?

_____

_____

_____

CHALLENGES: It was at this turning point today that I started to see progress.

_____

_____

_____

KINDNESS: One kind & loving statement I can say to myself after a difficult day.

_____

_____

_____

4. Wednesday

PRESENCE: Feeling into just this present moment, I notice...

INTENTION: I will connect back into feeling the present moment during these kinds of stressful/busy times today.

RESOURCES: Today I can take small and gentle steps towards...

POSITIVES: What positive outcome today made me feel supported or cared for?

CHALLENGES: A wonderful way to recharge during or at the end of a challenging day.

KINDNESS: To nurture more self-acceptance in my thoughts tomorrow I will...

---

5. Thursday

PRESENCE: The sensations I notice in my surroundings—temperature, texture, light...

_____

_____

INTENTION: I can remain calm when I encounter these... challenges today.

_____

_____

RESOURCES: A negative belief or behaviour pattern I can observe & gently question today.

_____

_____

_____

POSITIVES: In what positive way did I handle stress or frustration today?

_____

_____

CHALLENGES: A recent difficulty helped me discover this new strength within myself.

_____

_____

KINDNESS: One negative thought I can let go of tonight, & the positive one I replace it with.

_____

_____

6. Friday

PRESENCE: In this quiet moment of stillness, the thought that is challenging me is...

_____
_____

INTENTION: When I observe this thought without attaching to it, it looks....
(colour/texture/temperature)

_____
_____

RESOURCES: I can bring my resilience & power to these... situations today.

_____
_____

POSITIVES: A recent challenge that has helped me grow & that I now feel grateful for.

_____
_____

CHALLENGES: What frustrated me the most about today, & how can I approach it differently next time?

_____
_____

KINDNESS: How did I honour my feelings today, & how can I do that more often?

_____
_____

7. Saturday

PRESENCE: Reflecting on the process of something I am doing, rather than the future outcome reminds me...

INTENTION: I can show myself love today by...

RESOURCES: I can plan to cultivate more peace in these... aspects of my day today.

POSITIVES: How did I make a positive impact on someone else's day today?

CHALLENGES: A creative solution I have found for a problem that I will use again.

KINDNESS: A kindness I have given to someone that I will give again.

8. Sunday

PRESENCE: When I imagine stepping back and observing my feelings flow this morning, I can describe it as...

___

___

___

INTENTION: At these times... my productivity slows, & but my worth always stays the same.

___

___

___

RESOURCES: What I can offer myself to feel calm & okay, during moments of frustration.

___

___

___

POSITIVES: What experience today made me feel content or fulfilled?

___

___

___

CHALLENGES: How can I approach tomorrow with a growth mindset?

___

___

___

KINDNESS: I embrace these unique qualities in others, & in myself.

___

___

___

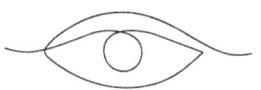

REFLECT
This week, what was the biggest lesson you learnt about balance?

___
___
___
___
___
___
___
___

REFOCUS
How can you adjust your schedule or mindset to create more balance next week?

___
___
___
___
___
___
___
___

9. Monday

PRESENCE: When I use deep breathing to relax; my body & mind feel...

INTENTION: My responsibilities today & my intended acts of self-care...

RESOURCES: My instincts are guiding me to....

POSITIVES: Someone I supported or listened to today, & the the gratitude it gives me.

CHALLENGES: An optimistic account of the challenges I have ahead of me.

KINDNESS: A habit or practice I can build that will reinforce positive self-talk in my daily life.

---

10. Tuesday

PRESENCE: A thought that I am curious about.

___
___
___

INTENTION: I can nurture peace in my mind today by...

___
___
___

RESOURCES: A strength I can use to help others today.

___
___
___

POSITIVES: What was the best part of my day, & why did it stand out?

___
___
___

CHALLENGES: The first thought I had when faced with a challenge today, & how it shaped my response.

___
___
___

KINDNESS: A thought & an action from today that offered kindness to myself or others:

___
___
___

11. Wednesday

PRESENCE: Feeling present now feels... I will use this resource at these... times/breaks/moments today.

INTENTION: Starting the day without putting unnecessary pressure on myself looks like...

RESOURCES: The actions I will take today to maintain my balance & calm...

POSITIVES: An experience today that opened my heart.

CHALLENGES: A fear or doubt, big or small, that I overcame today.

KINDNESS: Who I have shown compassion towards recently, how it felt, & when I can show myself the same.

12. Thursday

PRESENCE: When I bring attention to my breathing right now, I notice...

_____
_____

INTENTION: There is room in my day here... to offer myself this same kindness I would to a friend.

_____
_____

RESOURCES: I have felt confident when... and I can use this feeling to maintain my confidence today when...

_____
_____

POSITIVES: What did I learn today that I am grateful for?

_____
_____

CHALLENGES: When I am patient with myself during challenging moments I notice.

_____
_____

KINDNESS: What is one way I can share kindness with others tomorrow?

_____
_____

13. Friday

PRESENCE: An emotion I am noticing moving through me this morning is...

___

INTENTION: My worth feels valued when...

___

RESOURCES: I have noted these triggers... I have for this emotion... and I will soothe/ calm myself mindfully through them by...

___

POSITIVES: A relationship I nurtured in a positive way today.

___

CHALLENGES: One way I successfully adapted to a situation today.

___

KINDNESS: One self-judgment I noticed today & a self-acceptance I can offer to replace it.

___

ns
14. Saturday

PRESENCE: What small detail of this morning can I focus on to bring myself into this moment?

_____
_____
_____

INTENTION: One way I can prioritize my mental & emotional health today.

_____
_____
_____

RESOURCES: These priorities I have today... can be supported by these resources I have...

_____
_____
_____
_____

POSITIVES: Something unexpected today that I am thankful for.

_____
_____
_____

CHALLENGES: A challenge that has given me motivation to improve.

_____
_____
_____

KINDNESS: Something kind I said/did for someone today.

_____
_____
_____

15. Sunday

PRESENCE: Being mindful of the natural world around me now, I feel....

INTENTION: When worry comes my way today, I can do this... to detach from it and feel ok.

RESOURCES: These personal strengths... will support the decisions I make today.

POSITIVES: One positive outcome of my actions today.

CHALLENGES: A challenge today that I enjoyed & hope more of the same lie ahead.

KINDNESS: In moments of stress or anxiety, I will offer these kind words in self-talk & to those around me:

R & R

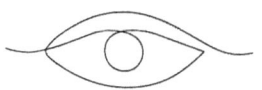

REFLECT
How did you handle conflict or difficult interactions this week?

_____
_____
_____
_____
_____
_____
_____
_____
_____

REFOCUS
What communication skills can you work on next week to foster healthier relationships?

_____
_____
_____
_____
_____
_____
_____
_____
_____

16. Monday

PRESENCE: I can observe my attention on the now, pulling it back from future worries or past ruminations feels...

_____

_____

_____

INTENTION: A task I can break down into smaller manageable steps today.

_____

_____

RESOURCES: In my day ahead, I will show myself compassion when...

_____

_____

_____

POSITIVES: What kindness did someone show me today that I appreciate?

_____

_____

CHALLENGES: One way I can stay patient & calm when challenges arise.

_____

_____

KINDNESS: Someone I would like to check in on more regularly.

_____

_____

_____

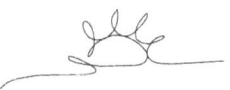

17. Tuesday

PRESENCE: I have noticed that bringing my attention to the present moment has these greater benefits for me.

_____

_____

_____

INTENTION: An act of self love I can take today.

_____

_____

_____

RESOURCES: Remaining centered in my strength today will allow me to be more open to....

_____

_____

_____

POSITIVES: How did I express or receive love & care today?

_____

_____

_____

CHALLENGES: A problem-solving technique that worked best for me today.

_____

_____

_____

KINDNESS: One thing I want to tell myself tonight to reinforce my sense of worthiness.

_____

_____

_____

18. Wednesday

PRESENCE: When I observe my inner world with curiosity instead of judgment, I notice...

_____

_____

_____

INTENTION: When I make mistakes today, I will offer this kindness to myself...

_____

_____

_____

RESOURCES: An area of my day I will navigate gracefully today.

_____

_____

_____

POSITIVES: One thing about my emotional or mental health that I feel grateful for today.

_____

_____

_____

CHALLENGES: A change I have embraced, even though it felt uncomfortable or difficult at first...

_____

_____

_____

KINDNESS: A flaw I've been hard on myself about, & a softened thought I offer now.

_____

_____

_____

19. Thursday

PRESENCE: Soft breath, deep breath, shallow breath: changing my breath, I notice...

INTENTION: What does a balanced, peaceful day look like for me today?

RESOURCES: What I can bring into my relationships & interactions today?

POSITIVES: A difficulty I am grateful I found the strength/courage to push through today.

CHALLENGES: How I can use that strength to approach tomorrow with more confidence.

KINDNESS: One practice I can use to cultivate more self-kindness in the days ahead.

---

20. Friday

PRESENCE: What does being present in conversations with others today look like & sound like?

___

INTENTION: A compassionate inner dialogue today starts with these words.

___

RESOURCES: When self-compassion & self-confidence coexist it feels like...

___

POSITIVES: What I feel the most thankful for today & how I can express that gratitude.

___

CHALLENGES: A lesson I have learnt that will help me stay positive in the future.

___

KINDNESS: Even when it's hard, I can speak kindly to myself, these are my fall back words of kindness...

21. Saturday

PRESENCE: Finding stillness in my mind brings me...

___

INTENTION: To help me approach challenges calmly & with clarity today, I will...

___

RESOURCES: I acknowledge these personal strengths as I start my day.

___

POSITIVES: One small thing that I might normally overlook but feel grateful for.

___

CHALLENGES: The emotions that came up for me at challenging times today.

___

KINDNESS: One positive thing I can say to myself right now to show kindness.

22. Sunday

PRESENCE: As I move or stretch my body this morning, the sensations I notice are...

_____

_____

_____

INTENTION: In difficult moments today, I will offer myself compassion by...

_____

_____

_____

RESOURCES: As I challenge myself today by... I will balance in self-care by...

_____

_____

_____

POSITIVES: How did I positively impact someone else's day today?

_____

_____

_____

CHALLENGES: A unique power I have discovered in myself.

_____

_____

_____

KINDNESS: A judgement I chose not to put on myself or someone else today.

_____

_____

_____

R & R

REFLECT
What boundary did you set this week, & how did it benefit you?

REFOCUS
What boundaries do you need to maintain or establish next week to protect your energy?

---

23. Monday

PRESENCE: I notice today, emotionally I am feeling... I can support, move through or prepare for these feelings today by...

___

___

___

INTENTION: When I feel myself comparing myself to others today I will...

___

___

___

RESOURCES: Something unique about me that I will carry confidently into the day.

___

___

___

POSITIVES: One thing about my community that I am grateful for today.

___

___

___

CHALLENGES: My approach to this challenge showed me I am stronger than I thought.

___

___

___

KINDNESS: How can I support myself (and loved ones) with more love & care during challenging times?

___

___

24. Tuesday

PRESENCE: The words I have to describe being present this morning.

INTENTION: Staying within my personal boundaries today looks like...

RESOURCES: A mindful practice I can use today & when it will be useful.

POSITIVES: How I practiced patience or understanding today, & how it affected my interactions?

CHALLENGES: A mistake I have resolved with flexibility or problem-solving skills.

KINDNESS: A loving act toward myself (or someone else) I can give tomorrow.

---

25. Wednesday

PRESENCE: When I use my breath to anchor myself in the present moment it helps...

_____

_____

INTENTION: I can avoid rushing through my day & stay balanced by...

_____

_____

RESOURCES: I can visualise myself in ease & flow at this often challenging time of the day.

_____

_____

POSITIVES: Something I relied on today that made my day easier.

_____

_____

CHALLENGES: A time I learnt to be brave in an uncertain situation.

_____

_____

KINDNESS: A mistake I have let go of and the lesson I have kept.

_____

_____

26. Thursday

PRESENCE: My description of a small, often unnoticed detail in my environment.

_____
_____
_____

INTENTION: When I feel my mind starting to overthink... I can tell myself...

_____
_____
_____

RESOURCES: I will use my compassion to support... (someone) through (something) today.

_____
_____
_____

POSITIVES: A small, comforting ritual or routine in my day that I am grateful for.

_____
_____
_____

CHALLENGES: The most empowering part of my day today.

_____
_____
_____

KINDNESS: What encouraging words can I use to support myself tomorrow?

_____
_____
_____

27. Friday

PRESENCE: A peaceful moment that quietens the mental noise today feels...

_____

_____

_____

INTENTION: When I start to feel distracted today, I can gently refocus myself by...

_____

_____

_____

RESOURCES: The best way to nurture productivity in my day today will be...

_____

_____

_____

POSITIVES: The joy or creativity I am grateful for today.

_____

_____

_____

CHALLENGES: The positive habits or practices that helped me reduce stress today.

_____

_____

_____

KINDNESS: One thing I can do tomorrow to support my emotional self-care.

_____

_____

_____

28. Saturday

PRESENCE: Breathing mindfully right now feels... & I can use this today when...

INTENTION: I can be kinder to myself when...

RESOURCES: One area of my day where I will try to balance being strong & being gentle with myself.

POSITIVES: Something comforting or reassuring about today that I am grateful for.

CHALLENGES: A moment when I got to practice thinking on my feet.

KINDNESS: Something I can do to make a positive difference to someone else tomorrow.

---

29. Sunday

PRESENCE: A common story I notice I am telling myself & a way I am rewriting it.

_____

_____

_____

INTENTION: When self-doubt appears today I can release it by...

_____

_____

_____

RESOURCES: A challenge coming for me today that I will use as a chance to grow...

_____

_____

_____

POSITIVES: Someone or something that made me smile today.

_____

_____

_____

CHALLENGES: Something I could & something I could not control today.

_____

_____

_____

KINDNESS: When I'm feeling less than perfect, I can show kindness to myself by...

_____

_____

_____

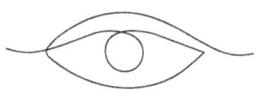

REFLECT
How did you surprise yourself with your resilience or resourcefulness this week?

REFOCUS
How can you continue to trust your inner strength in the week ahead?

---

30. Monday

PRESENCE: Savouring this moment... it looks, feels, sounds, tastes, smells like...

INTENTION: My day ahead in self-acceptance & peace could feel...

RESOURCES: I can make confident, aligned choices today when...

POSITIVES: A positive thought or attitude I want to carry with me into tomorrow.

CHALLENGES: One way I can practice positivity when facing a challenge.

KINDNESS: Did I notice my self-talk improving today, & what can I do to continue?

Building Strength from Within

As the coldest month of the year, July is a time to focus on building inner strength. Visualise yourself as a tree with deep roots that remain strong & stable, even in the midst of winter's challenges. What inner resources—such as resilience, patience, or determination—can you draw on this month? See yourself cultivating these qualities through intentional actions & self-reflection. Imagine how this inner strength will support you, not only through winter but throughout the rest of the year.

Self Care Bingo

How many can you tick today?

Used an Affirmation	Connected with a Friend	Meditated 10 mins
Enjoyed a Bath or Shower	Got Some Fresh Air	Ate a Healthy Meal
Read a Book or Listened to Music	Stopped to Breathe	Wrote in Your Journal
Drank Water	Early to Bed or Day Napped	Encouraged or Complimented Yourself
Moved Your Body	Gave a Random Act of Kindness to Someone	Set a Boundary

1. Tuesday

PRESENCE: What thoughts are taking up space in my mind, & how can I soften them?

INTENTION: What does a calm & peaceful day look like for me?

RESOURCES: When can I choose to feel strong today?

POSITIVES: A natural beauty or environment around me that I noticed today.

CHALLENGES: A learning experience I had today.

KINDNESS: How can I be more loving toward myself when things are difficult?

---

2. Wednesday

PRESENCE: Tuning in to my body, I notice it needs... today.

_____

_____

_____

INTENTION: If I have any moments of doubt today, I can offer this mantra of self-acceptance.

_____

_____

_____

RESOURCES: How can I be my own best supporter today?

_____

_____

_____

POSITIVES: A small, joyful moment I experienced today.

_____

_____

_____

CHALLENGES: What future challenges do I look forward to embracing?

_____

_____

_____

KINDNESS: My imperfections are perfect for me in this way...

_____

_____

_____

3. Thursday

PRESENCE: Am I noticing any uncomfortable emotions, & can I simply observe them?

INTENTION: Some learning I intend to gather through my day today.

RESOURCES: At these choice points today I can let my self-awareness inform my decisions & behaviours.

POSITIVES: What freedom or choice today am I thankful for?

CHALLENGES: What mindset helped me push through the toughest part of today?

KINDNESS: What is one way I can transform self-criticism into self-encouragement tomorrow?

---

4. Friday

PRESENCE: How can I invite a sense of stillness & mindfulness into this day?

INTENTION: I will respect my own energy levels during these times today.

RESOURCES: Observing my inner dialogue today, I can shift it in this empowering direction...

POSITIVES: What positive changes have I noticed in myself over this time?

CHALLENGES: What lessons learned from today can I embrace & apply tomorrow?

KINDNESS: How can I be more patient & accepting of my personal journey & growth?

---

5. Saturday

PRESENCE: Often the space around me reflects the way I feel, so how can I use this knowledge to support myself?

___
___
___

INTENTION: I can make space for joy & self-acceptance in these ways today.

___
___
___

RESOURCES: I can use both strength & mindfulness to face this challenge today.

___
___
___

POSITIVES: What made my day feel easier or more manageable?

___
___
___

CHALLENGES: One way I can release any remaining stress from today before I go to bed.

___
___
___

KINDNESS: One way I can make speaking kindly to myself a daily habit.

___
___
___

6. Sunday

PRESENCE: What thoughts are present for me this morning?

INTENTION: How could I remain calm in my mind today?

RESOURCES: Which of my personal strengths could be my focus today?

POSITIVES: What was a moment today that made me feel proud of myself?

CHALLENGES: How did I initially respond to the biggest challenge of my day?

KINDNESS: What is one kind thing I did for myself today?

REFLECT
How did you prioritize your well-being this week?

_____
_____
_____
_____
_____
_____
_____
_____

REFOCUS
What's one self-care practice you want to commit to next week?

_____
_____
_____
_____
_____
_____
_____
_____

7. Monday

PRESENCE: What distractions are pulling me away from the present moment right now, & how can I let them go?

_____

_____

_____

INTENTION: In what ways can I practice patience with myself today?

_____

_____

RESOURCES: How can I balance my desire for growth with the need to be kind to myself today?

_____

_____

_____

POSITIVES: What is something I did today that I feel proud & thankful for?

_____

_____

CHALLENGES: What strength did I rely on to get through challenges today?

_____

_____

KINDNESS: How did I take care of my emotional well-being today, & how can I continue to do so?

_____

_____

_____

8. Tuesday

PRESENCE: How can I approach my tasks today with more presence & awareness?

INTENTION: How can I show myself love & care today?

RESOURCES: How can I maintain a sense of inner calm today, while also leaning into my strengths?

POSITIVES: How did I feel connected to others in a meaningful way today?

CHALLENGES. A challenge today allow me to practice my problem-solving skills.

KINDNESS: What did I do today that made me feel proud of myself?

---

9. Wednesday

PRESENCE: With eyes closed, my mind feels...

___
___
___

INTENTION: Where in my day can I quiet the inner critic & trust myself more?

___
___
___

RESOURCES: How can I respond to challenges today with more awareness & mindfulness?

___
___
___

POSITIVES: What is one thing about my life today that brings me peace or comfort?

___
___
___

CHALLENGES: How were my challenges important to my personal growth?

___
___
___

KINDNESS: How can I show kindness to myself when I make a mistake?

___
___
___

10. Thursday

PRESENCE: Focusing on the rhythm of my breath, how does it feel?

INTENTION: What can I do today to feel more balanced & centred?

RESOURCES: How can I use my self awareness to approach today with more clarity?

POSITIVES: What is one thing I accomplished today, big or small, that I am proud of?

CHALLENGES: What obstacles today helped me build confidence in my abilities?

KINDNESS: The self-compassion of today that I will carry into tomorrow.

---

11. Friday

PRESENCE: Sitting with the here & now, the sensations I observe are...

INTENTION: What supports can I use to enter this day with an open heart & mind?

RESOURCES: What growth am I experiencing, & how can I nurture it?

POSITIVES: What am I most grateful for today, & why does it matter to me?

CHALLENGES: How can I end the day feeling positive about the challenges I faced?

KINDNESS: How did I improve my self-talk today, & what can I do to keep progressing?

---

12. Saturday

PRESENCE: Observing my thoughts without judgement feels like...

_____
_____
_____

INTENTION: One thing I can do to stay calm during stressful moments today is...

_____
_____
_____

RESOURCES: How can I build on the resilience I have shown?

_____
_____
_____

POSITIVES: What is one interaction or conversation that had a positive impact on me today?

_____
_____
_____

CHALLENGES: How did today's challenges make me feel, & why?

_____
_____
_____

KINDNESS: In what ways can I be gentler with myself in moments of frustration?

_____
_____

13. Sunday

PRESENCE: As I scan my body this morning I notice it feels...

INTENTION: What does it look like to forgive myself if things don't go as planned today?

RESOURCES: How can I move forward today with confidence in my abilities?

POSITIVES: What is something I own that I felt grateful to have today?

CHALLENGES: What positive outcomes could come from the challenges today?

KINDNESS: A self-critical thought I had today, & it's replacement in self-compassion.

R & R

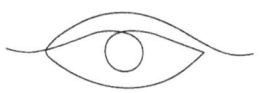

REFLECT
What risk did you take this week that moved you out of your comfort zone?

_____
_____
_____
_____
_____
_____
_____
_____
_____

REFOCUS
How can you continue embracing discomfort for growth next week?

_____
_____
_____
_____
_____
_____
_____
_____
_____

14. Monday

PRESENCE: What emotions can I observe, without getting caught up in them?

INTENTION: What would self-acceptance feel like as I move through today?

RESOURCES: Today I will observe with curiosity my response to these challenges...

POSITIVES: How did I practice kindness toward myself today?

CHALLENGES: How was I pushed outside my comfort zone, & what did I learn?

KINDNESS: When can I practice more positive self-talk when I feel self-critical?

15. Tuesday

PRESENCE: I can ground myself before beginning the tasks of the day by...

INTENTION: One boundary I can set today to protect my peace is...

RESOURCES: A choice I can make today to support balance for my mind &/or body.

POSITIVES: What is one skill or ability I used today that I am thankful for?

CHALLENGES: A setback I faced today that I can turn into a lesson for the future.

KINDNESS: What is one part of myself that I want to embrace with more acceptance?

---

16. Wednesday

PRESENCE: My observations of the sights & sounds surrounding me.

___
___

INTENTION: One small thing I can let go of today that is causing me stress.

___
___

RESOURCES: One way I can acknowledge my strengths today (without needing validation from others)?

___
___

POSITIVES: What did I do today to strengthen a relationship, & how did it feel?

___
___

CHALLENGES: How did I demonstrate resilience today?

___
___

KINDNESS: I can replace this negative thought with this uplifting one tomorrow.

___
___

17. Thursday

PRESENCE: A calm space in my mind feels like...

INTENTION: One way I can embrace the flow of the day without rushing through it...

RESOURCES: I can enjoy growth today without pushing myself too hard by...

POSITIVES: Who helped me feel more positive or supported today?

CHALLENGES: How can I improve the way I handle frustration when facing difficulties?

KINDNESS: Tomorrow I can show more emotional care toward myself by...

---

18. Friday

PRESENCE: Focusing fully on each task without distraction today will feel...

INTENTION: I will celebrate my uniqueness & individuality today by...

RESOURCES: Balancing my strength & inner peace today looks like...

POSITIVES: Which challenging situation positively impacted my day?

CHALLENGES: What creative solutions did I come up with today?

KINDNESS: I can remind myself of my worth, even when I am deeply challenged by...

---

19. Saturday

PRESENCE: One feeling or sensation I observe this morning...

_____

_____

_____

INTENTION: Where in my day can I see room to be less hard on myself?

_____

_____

_____

RESOURCES: At these times today... I can remind myself that I have everything I need within me to navigate challenges.

_____

_____

_____

POSITIVES: What is one way in which today's events unfolded that I am thankful for?

_____

_____

_____

CHALLENGES: What did today's difficulty teach me about adapting to change?

_____

_____

_____

KINDNESS: What imperfection did I notice in myself today, & how can I embrace it with love?

_____

_____

_____

20. Sunday

PRESENCE: How it feels to take a deep, mindful breath & pause right now.

_____

_____

INTENTION: I can maintain a balance between work & rest today by...

_____

_____

RESOURCES: What do I know about myself that will support my tasks & interactions today?

_____

_____

_____

POSITIVES: How did I stay focused & productive today, & what made that possible?

_____

_____

CHALLENGES: What have I learnt about stepping into discomfort with courage?

_____

_____

KINDNESS: What is one thing I can let go of tonight in order to show myself more kindness tomorrow?

_____

_____

R & R

REFLECT
How did you practice mindfulness or stay present this week?

_____
_____
_____
_____
_____
_____
_____
_____

REFOCUS
How can you remain more mindful or connected to the present moment next week?

_____
_____
_____
_____
_____
_____
_____
_____

21. Monday

PRESENCE: What does it feel like to breathe in this moment & release the need to plan or worry about the rest of the day?

___

___

___

INTENTION: What does self-compassion look like for me as I start this day?

___

___

RESOURCES: I can remind myself that growth often comes from stepping outside of my comfort zone when...

___

___

___

POSITIVES: Who made me feel valued today, & why am I grateful for it?

___

___

___

CHALLENGES: One positive from today's challenge that I want to remember...

___

___

___

KINDNESS: A self-critical thought I'd like to challenge & replace with a positive one:

___

___

___

22. Tuesday

PRESENCE: What is my mind focusing on at this moment, & how does it affect me?

___

INTENTION: A kind & compassionate thought I can use for myself today.

___

RESOURCES: One way I can rely on my inner strength to navigate challenges today.

___

POSITIVES: What is one thing today that I am truly grateful for?

___

CHALLENGES: The hardest part of today, & what I learnt about myself from facing it.

___

KINDNESS: One kind thought I want to tell myself before bed tonight.

___

23. Wednesday

PRESENCE: Listening closely to the signals my body is sending me, I notice...

INTENTION: Where in my day can I offer compassion to myself?

RESOURCES: One area where I'd like to deepen my self-awareness today...

POSITIVES: What positive habit did I follow through with today, & how did it make me feel?

CHALLENGES: What did I gain from the challenges today that I didn't expect?

KINDNESS: What I forgive myself for today (no matter how small).

24. Thursday

PRESENCE: *I gently check in with my emotions and feel...*

___
___
___

INTENTION: *When can I remind myself that I am enough, exactly as I am today?*

___
___

RESOURCES: *What is one challenge I can face with strength & self-compassion today?*

___
___
___

POSITIVES: *What is something about my home that I appreciate today?*

___
___

CHALLENGES: *One small win I experienced today.*

___
___
___

KINDNESS: *How did I practice self-acceptance today, & what did it feel like?*

___
___
___

25. Friday

PRESENCE: The temperature of my breath this morning feels...

_____

_____

_____

INTENTION: I can stay in tune with my emotional needs today by...

_____

_____

_____

RESOURCES: Today, I can focus on aligning with this personal value of mine.

_____

_____

_____

POSITIVES: How did I balance productivity & rest today in a way that felt good?

_____

_____

_____

CHALLENGES: What can I improve on the next time I encounter a challenge like the one I had today?

_____

_____

_____

KINDNESS: An affirming statement I can tell myself to reinforce my self-worth.

_____

_____

_____

26. Saturday

PRESENCE: The things I see, hear, feel, touch, taste in the world around me right now.

_____

_____

INTENTION: I can describe this plan to take a break if I feel overwhelmed today.

_____

_____

RESOURCES: How I can stay true to myself, when faced with opposition or difficulty today.

_____

_____

_____

POSITIVES: Who made my day easier or more enjoyable, & how can I show them gratitude?

_____

_____

CHALLENGES: How can I build on the flexibility I have shown when faced with a challenge?

_____

_____

KINDNESS: I can be more patient with myself when I'm feeling overwhelmed by...

_____

_____

27. Sunday

PRESENCE: One thought or concern I can set aside to focus on the present is...

INTENTION: What does it look like to stay present today?

RESOURCES: How can I pace my day productively & avoid feeling rushed?

POSITIVES: How did I respond to a situation today that showed growth in my mindset or behaviour?

CHALLENGES: What have I learnt about staying calm & centred during stressful moments?

KINDNESS: What is one way I can boost my sense of self-worth tomorrow?

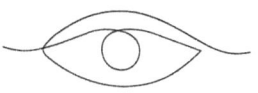

REFLECT
How did you inspire or motivate someone else this week?

___

REFOCUS
How can you continue to lift others up & spread positivity next week?

___

28. Monday

PRESENCE: Feeling into the soles of my feet this morning, I notice...?

___
___
___

INTENTION: One thing I can do to prioritise my well-being today.

___
___

RESOURCES: How can I use my strength to create more peace & harmony in my day?

___
___
___

POSITIVES: Who am I thankful for being in my life today, & why?

___
___
___

CHALLENGES: A creative response I have had to a challenging situation.

___
___
___

KINDNESS: I am learning to be compassionate toward these beautiful flaws & imperfections.

___
___
___

29. Tuesday

PRESENCE: When I feel my mind is wandering, I gently bring it back to the present by...

___

___

___

INTENTION: I can remind myself that I am are worthy of kindness & understanding with these words...

___

___

___

RESOURCES: How can I respond, rather than react, to difficulties today?

___

___

___

POSITIVES: What is one way I made time for self-care today, & how did it enhance my mood?

___

___

CHALLENGES: How did I adapt in the day, & what did I learn from adapting?

___

___

___

KINDNESS: I can offer myself more compassion tomorrow by...

___

___

___

30. Wednesday

PRESENCE: When I breathe deeply & consciously I notice...

INTENTION: How can I create more peace in my day today?

RESOURCES: How can I use what I know of my self to improve this day?

POSITIVES: What is one accomplishment from today that I am grateful for?

CHALLENGES: The confidence I gained today, & how I will carry it into future challenges.

KINDNESS: One affirmation I can repeat to myself tomorrow to encourage positive self-talk.

---

31. Thursday

PRESENCE: Focusing on the sound of my breath, I notice...

INTENTION: One way I can approach today with ease & self-kindness is...

RESOURCES: I can act with both confidence & compassion towards myself & others today when...

POSITIVES: What positive feelings am I taking with me into tomorrow?

CHALLENGES: Rather than these setbacks, I can focus on this progress I made today.

KINDNESS: What is one thing I can forgive myself for today?

Squashing ANTs

Squash your Automatic Negative Thoughts with Positive Replacement Thoughts.

Write any ANT's that you can think of in the column to the left. Consider each one & see if you can challenge it with a Positive Replacement in the right column

You can return to this page & continue to work on your reframes.

AUTOMATIC NEGATIVE THOUGHT	POSITIVE REPLACEMENT THOUGHT
I can't do this	I can break this down into smaller manageable steps

Reawakening and Renewal

As the first hints of spring appear, visualise yourself awakening to new possibilities. Picture the buds of spring starting to bloom around you, symbolising fresh ideas, opportunities, & energy. What parts of your life are ready to blossom? See yourself stepping into this renewal with excitement, setting clear intentions for personal or professional growth. Describe the buds and blooms of new growth unfolding around you. Imagine how this sense of renewal can carry you forward with purpose & enthusiasm.

1. Friday

PRESENCE: I gently redirect to the present moment when my mind wanders & notice...

___
___
___

INTENTION: What would it feel like to go through the day with a peaceful mindset?

___
___
___

RESOURCES: I can remind myself of my strengths when faced with these kinds of difficulties today.

___
___
___

POSITIVES: Which person am I thankful for today, & why?

___
___
___

CHALLENGES: Which challenge offered me an opportunity for growth today?

___
___
___

KINDNESS: How did I take care of my emotional well-being today?

___
___
___

2. Saturday

PRESENCE: What is my body asking for right now—rest, movement, nourishment, or something else?

___

___

___

INTENTION: Responding to mistakes with patience today, looks like...

___

___

___

RESOURCES: How I want to feel at the end of today, & how I can encourage it?

___

___

___

POSITIVES: What made me smile or laugh today,?

___

___

___

CHALLENGES: How could today's challenge be preparing me for future situations?

___

___

___

KINDNESS: My struggles & imperfections, and the understanding I offer them.

___

___

___

3. Sunday

PRESENCE: Checking in with my emotions, I notice I feel...

___

INTENTION: What would it look like to accept my emotions today, even the uncomfortable ones?

___

RESOURCES: I can check on my thoughts & feelings during these situations today...

___

POSITIVES: What is one piece of good news or positivity that came my way today?

___

CHALLENGES: How did I stay grounded when dealing with difficulty today?

___

KINDNESS: Tomorrow I can remind myself that it's okay to be imperfect by...

___

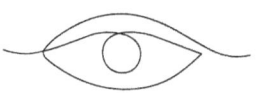

REFLECT
How did you stay aligned with your core values this week?

_____
_____
_____
_____
_____
_____
_____
_____
_____

REFOCUS
What further actions can you take next week to continue being true to yourself?

_____
_____
_____
_____
_____
_____
_____
_____
_____

4. Monday

PRESENCE: When I deepen my breath into my belly, I feel...

_____

_____

INTENTION: I can communicate my needs to others clearly today when...

_____

_____

RESOURCES: I can reflect my values through these actions today.

_____

_____

POSITIVES: What made me feel connected to others today?

_____

_____

CHALLENGES: In a difficult situation I can be compassionate toward myself by...

_____

_____

KINDNESS: The best way I can remind myself that I am enough, just as I am.

_____

_____

_____

5. Tuesday

PRESENCE: When I close my eyes and release the clutter in my mind it looks...

___

___

___

INTENTION: I can remain grounded in the face of stress today by...

___

___

___

RESOURCES: Some actions I can take today to reflect my strength & resolve are...

___

___

___

POSITIVES: What is something today that reminded me of the goodness in life?

___

___

___

CHALLENGES: What resources did I use today to help me stay strong during challenges?

___

___

___

KINDNESS: When things don't go as planned, I can remind myself of these kind words.

___

___

___

6. Wednesday

PRESENCE: One thing I can notice in my environment that I've not paid attention to before.

___

___

INTENTION: In which spaces can I remind myself to pause & breathe today?

___

___

RESOURCES: I can navigate the priorites today with a sense of ease by...

___

___

___

POSITIVES: One thing that went smoothly or easily for me today.

___

___

CHALLENGES: What positive coping mechanisms do I have for stressful challenges?

___

___

___

KINDNESS: What emotion did I allow myself to feel fully today, without judgment?

___

___

___

7. Thursday

PRESENCE: While eating breakfast slowly & mindfully, I notice...

INTENTION: I can nurture my emotions today by...

RESOURCES: In what situations can I use inner calm to anchor my strength today?

POSITIVES: What resource or opportunity was I grateful for today?

CHALLENGES: How have my critical thinking skills helped with a challenge?

KINDNESS: My worth extends beyond my achievements or productivity. I know I have these positive qualities.

---

8. Friday

PRESENCE: Is there a thought pattern I am noticing that I can choose not to engage with today?

_____

_____

_____

INTENTION: One thing I can do to create balance in my relationships today is...

_____

_____

_____

RESOURCES: In today's potential challenges, I will use this mindful approach.

_____

_____

_____

POSITIVES: What friendship am I grateful for, & why?

_____

_____

_____

CHALLENGES: An experience I've had that has taught me a better version of myself.

_____

_____

_____

KINDNESS: Which area of my life needs more self-compassion practice?

_____

_____

_____

9. Saturday

PRESENCE: The movement of my breath today feels...

___
___
___

INTENTION: What does loving my imperfections look & sound like today?

___
___

RESOURCES: When I act in alignment with my values it feels...

___
___
___

POSITIVES: What is one resource or tool that helped me succeed today?

___
___

CHALLENGES: When have I trusted myself through a decision or challenge, & how did it feel?

___
___
___

KINDNESS: What can I do tomorrow to continue practicing self-kindness in difficult moments?

___
___
___

10. Sunday

PRESENCE: Feeling present and releasing worry about the future feels...

INTENTION: One way I can respond to myself with empathy today...

RESOURCES: When I trust in myself, decisions today look...

POSITIVES: Where did I respond with positivity or strength today?

CHALLENGES: What lessons from today can I use to create a better tomorrow?

KINDNESS: Where can I put more loving & supportive self-talk into my daily routine?

R & R

REFLECT
How did you handle change or unexpected events this week?

___

REFOCUS
How can you better adapt to change & embrace flexibility next week?

___

11. Monday

PRESENCE: When I close my eyes and breathe kindly, I see...

INTENTION: Where/when can I slow down & enjoy the present moment today?

RESOURCES: One challenge I have overcome that proves my ability to grow is...

POSITIVES: What opportunity or experience today am I most thankful for?

CHALLENGES: What did today reveal about my strengths or weaknesses?

KINDNESS: One small act of self-kindness I can do for myself tomorrow.

12. Tuesday

PRESENCE: This morning my energy levels in my body are...

_____

_____

INTENTION: I can remember to speak to myself kindly today when...

_____

_____

RESOURCES: What small step toward growth can I take today, even if it feels uncomfortable?

_____

_____

POSITIVES: What was the most peaceful or calming moment of my day?

_____

_____

CHALLENGES: The challenges & valuable learning experiences I had today...

_____

_____

KINDNESS: When did I show myself compassion, & how did it feel?

_____

_____

13. Wednesday

PRESENCE: What emotions am I noticing this morning?

___

___

___

INTENTION: In what ways can I let go of the need to be perfect today?

___

___

___

RESOURCES: I can check in with my needs & emotions today by...

___

___

___

POSITIVES: What is one strength or skill I used today that I am thankful for?

___

___

___

CHALLENGES: What strategy worked well for me in harder moments today?

___

___

___

KINDNESS: I challenged this negative thought with this positive self-talk replacement.

___

___

___

14. Thursday

PRESENCE: When I observe the sensations in my relaxed hands, I notice...

INTENTION: One thing I can say "no" to today for my own well-being.

RESOURCES: I know myself well enough to know that today I will need this resource.

POSITIVES: One thing I learned today that will help me grow in a positive direction.

CHALLENGES: One thing I would do differently if I could redo a challenge in my day.

KINDNESS: One thing I did today that I completely accept without judgment.

15. Friday

PRESENCE: Right now, in my surroundings I am noticing...

INTENTION: One way I can make things easier for myself today.

RESOURCES: One boundary I can assert in a kind, yet firm, way today.

POSITIVES: What positive memory from today do I want to cherish?

CHALLENGES: I can celebrate the strength I showed at difficult times today by...

KINDNESS: What is one positive affirmation I want to focus on for tomorrow?

16. Saturday

PRESENCE: When I still my mind, I find I can let go of this worry easily...

_____
_____
_____

INTENTION: I can notice my reactions today with compassion and soothe myself by...

_____
_____
_____

RESOURCES: I can see myself pause & reflect before reacting to these kinds of difficult situations today.

_____
_____
_____

POSITIVES: One positive decision I made today that I want to continue making.

_____
_____
_____

CHALLENGES: What self-care practices could have helped me during stressful times today?

_____
_____
_____

KINDNESS: How can I show myself more kindness when I'm feeling emotionally vulnerable?

_____
_____
_____

17. Sunday

PRESENCE: When I am fully present for my morning cuppa today, I notice...

_____

_____

_____

INTENTION: One way I can honour my body & its needs today.

_____

_____

RESOURCES: When difficulty shows up today, I will remain peaceful & strong by...

_____

_____

_____

POSITIVES: What is one thing I often take for granted that I felt thankful for today?

_____

_____

CHALLENGES: Today encouraged me to find this new way to approach a problem.

_____

_____

_____

KINDNESS: The positive qualities I see in myself today, & how I can celebrate them.

_____

_____

_____

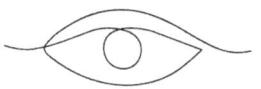

REFLECT
How did you practice patience or persistence this week?

___

REFOCUS
What goal can you approach with renewed persistence next week?

18. Monday

PRESENCE: When I am patient and curious about my present thoughts, I notice...

_____

_____

INTENTION: When I notice negative self-talk today, I will...

_____

_____

RESOURCES: One way I can be kind to myself today.

_____

_____

_____

POSITIVES: What is one thing I did to protect my energy or maintain balance today?

_____

_____

CHALLENGES: One way I may have grown through a situation/challenge today.

_____

_____

KINDNESS: The mistakes I made today, and why they are okay.

_____

_____

_____

19. Tuesday

PRESENCE: Focusing on my breath, I notice...

INTENTION: Where can I cultivate more harmony in my environment today?

RESOURCES: When I remain calm in the choices I make today, I can feel...

POSITIVES: What positive feedback or recognition did I receive today?

CHALLENGES: These are the successes I choose to remember when I face future difficulties.

KINDNESS: What unrealistic expectation of myself can I lift from my day tomorrow...

---

ns
20. Wednesday

PRESENCE: When I relax my mind and calm my thoughts it feels...

INTENTION: The qualities I have that I will let myself feel guided by today are...

RESOURCES: I can find confidence to approach these tasks today.

POSITIVES: What is one action I want to repeat because of its positive impact?

CHALLENGES: A challenge that passed me today and the learning I will keep from it.

KINDNESS: As I improve how I speak to myself - I hear myself saying...

21. Thursday

PRESENCE: This morning my heart/soul feels...

_____

_____

INTENTION: How I can bring more calm into my interactions today.

_____

_____

RESOURCES: As I am noticing my power, things feel...

_____

_____

POSITIVES: How did I step outside of my comfort zone in a positive way today?

_____

_____

CHALLENGES: What challenge have I overcome that boosted my confidence?

_____

_____

KINDNESS: When I'm feeling overwhelmed, I will offer myself these kind words.

_____

_____

22. Friday

PRESENCE: What part of my body feels the most relaxed, & what part feels tense?

___

___

INTENTION: One way I can show myself understanding today.

___

___

RESOURCES: One way I can move myself towards my goals.

___

___

POSITIVES: Who supported or helped me today, & how can I show gratitude?

___

___

CHALLENGES: One thing I could have done differently to make today easier on me.

___

___

KINDNESS: When I'm struggling, I will remind myself...

___

___

23. Saturday

PRESENCE: A feeling I am moving through, and how I will gently support myself.

_____

_____

_____

INTENTION: Something I would like to improve on or learn today.

_____

_____

_____

RESOURCES: Where/when can I take my time & respond more thoughtfully today?

_____

_____

_____

POSITIVES: What interaction had a positive affect on my day?

_____

_____

_____

CHALLENGES: Overcoming a challenge makes me feel...

_____

_____

_____

KINDNESS: How did I move away from self-doubt & show myself love today?

_____

_____

_____

24. Sunday

PRESENCE: When I slow down & savour the sensations of this moment, it feels...

INTENTION: In what way will I listen & respond to my body's needs today?

RESOURCES: What actions can I take today that align with my values & intentions?

POSITIVES: What am I most grateful for about the timing of events in my day?

CHALLENGES: The mistakes I made & what I learnt from them.

KINDNESS: How I can accept & celebrate my efforts of the day.

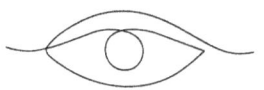

REFLECT
What positive impact did you have on others this week?

_____
_____
_____
_____
_____
_____
_____
_____
_____

REFOCUS
How can you contribute in a positive way to those around you next week?

_____
_____
_____
_____
_____
_____
_____
_____
_____

25. Monday

PRESENCE: How the space I am in affects my mood, & what I notice about it right now.

___
___
___

INTENTION: One way I can release any tension in my body today.

___
___

RESOURCES: In situations that would typically cause stress today, I remain calm & strong by...

___
___
___

POSITIVES: The positive emotion I experienced the most today, & what created it.

___
___

CHALLENGES: A challenge that taught me about my ability to persevere recently was.

___
___
___

KINDNESS: The kind words that uplifted me today, & where I will use them again.

___
___
___

26. Tuesday

PRESENCE: What is happening around me in this moment now?

___
___
___

INTENTION: One way I can be fully present in my tasks today.

___
___
___

RESOURCES: An area where I can gently push myself out of my comfort zone today.

___
___
___

POSITIVES: What is one thing about my environment today that I felt grateful for?

___
___
___

CHALLENGES: In what ways have I shown I can handle stress better than I thought?

___
___
___

KINDNESS: Tomorrow, I can nurture my emotional needs with compassion by...

___
___
___

27. Wednesday

PRESENCE: 5 slow, deep, belly breaths make me feel...

___
___
___

INTENTION: Who will I practice present and open communication with today?

___
___

RESOURCES: I will tune into my self-talk during these vulnerable spaces today... & offer these supportive words instead...

___
___
___

POSITIVES: How did I contribute positively to the people/group around me today?

___
___

CHALLENGES: An unexpected solution I found during a challenge.

___
___
___

KINDNESS: Did I acknowledge my self-worth today, & how can I ensure I do so tomorrow?

___
___

28. Thursday

PRESENCE: The thoughts I am having right now are... without judgement.

INTENTION: I can remind myself that I am doing the best I can today, when...

RESOURCES: It will be useful to stay present & centered when I am facing/doing this today.

POSITIVES: What positive surprise did today bring that I am grateful for?

CHALLENGES: I adapted when this happened today.

KINDNESS: An imperfection/mistake I can reframe with kindness.

---

29. Friday

PRESENCE: Taking a few moments of stillness to connect with my breath feels...

INTENTION: Today I can maintain a calm & balanced attitude when...

RESOURCES: At these difficult times today... I can focus on this growth it offers me...

POSITIVES: One way I maintained motivation throughout the day.

CHALLENGES: A moment that showed me I am capable of more than I thought.

KINDNESS: What is one thing I can tell myself tonight to ease any worries or self-doubt?

---

30. Saturday

PRESENCE: Letting the past be passed & focusing on right now, I notice...

___

INTENTION: At these times, I will choose to be gentle with myself by...

___

RESOURCES: I will choose self-confidence & self-belief today when...

___

POSITIVES: One inspiring thing I noticed today.

___

CHALLENGES: A positive mindset shift I have noticed in myself.

___

KINDNESS: A kindness I gave to someone today.

31. Sunday

PRESENCE: A thought pattern I am observing myself have.

_____
_____

INTENTION: I can encourage a calm environment in my home/workspace today by...

_____
_____

RESOURCES: I choose to stand confidently in my strengths today when...

_____
_____

POSITIVES: What positive outcome or solution did I find today that made me feel good?

_____
_____

CHALLENGES: A resource or support I use to handle challenging moments.

_____
_____

KINDNESS: Something I did today that deserves self-praise or acknowledgment.

_____
_____

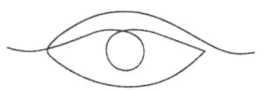

REFLECT
How did you challenge yourself this week, & what did you learn from it?

_____
_____
_____
_____
_____
_____
_____
_____

REFOCUS
How can you continue stepping outside your comfort zone next week?

_____
_____
_____
_____
_____
_____
_____

More Words for You

Highlight the affirmations that feel right for you, or close your eyes and let your finger land on one to use today!

Self-Acceptance & Authenticity:

- I am free to be myself.
- I embrace who I am, inside & out.
- I accept myself fully & completely.
- I am proud of who I am becoming.
- I love who I am & what I offer the world.
- I am comfortable in my own skin.
- I honor my unique gifts & talents.
- I trust my intuition & my inner wisdom.
- I am enough, just as I am.
- I trust myself & the path I am on.

Growth & Progress:

- I celebrate my progress, no matter how small.
- I am open to new ideas & perspectives.
- I am a work in progress, & I am proud of my journey.
- I embrace change as a positive force in my life.
- I learn from my mistakes & grow stronger.
- I believe in my ability to improve & grow.
- I am open to new opportunities & challenges.

Inner Peace & Calm:

- I trust in the flow of life.
- I am at peace with where I am in life.
- I choose peace over worry.
- I release the need for control & trust the process.
- I create a calm & peaceful environment around me.
- I am centered, calm, & in control of my emotions.
- I am at peace with who I am.
- I attract peace & harmony into my life.
- I choose to let go of what I cannot change.
- I am grounded, centered, & stable.

Body Positivity & Self-Care:

- I honor & respect my body as it is today.
- I am grateful for everything my body allows me to experience & achieve.
- I nourish my body with kindness, love, & patience.
- I release all comparison & celebrate my unique beauty.
- I treat my body with respect & care, listening to its needs.
- I am strong, capable, & deserving of self-love.
- I let go of self-criticism & embrace compassion toward myself.
- My body is a beautiful home, & I am grateful for it.

September

Planting Seeds of Growth

With spring in full bloom, visualise yourself reseeding for future growth. Picture a garden that represents your goals, aspirations, & personal development. What new seeds are you planting now that will grow & move you towards the meaningful achievements or changes you desire for the coming month? See yourself nurturing these successive seeds with care, patience, & attention. Imagine how your consistent efforts, no matter how small, build towards future success & fulfillment. Visualise the growth that comes from the seeds cultivated now.

1. Monday

PRESENCE: Staying connected to my body as I move through today will feel...

INTENTION: I can ease up on self-criticism today when...

RESOURCES: To welcome & be open to new opportunities today I will...

POSITIVES: A simple pleasure, (e.g. favorite meal or activity) am I grateful for today.

CHALLENGES: This challenge helped me grow today.

KINDNESS: A moment today I could treat myself with the same compassion I would offer a friend in a similar situation.

---

2. Tuesday

PRESENCE: Where I am holding emotion in my body right now, & how I can release it gently today.

INTENTION: The strengths & weaknesses I choose to acknowledge & accept today.

RESOURCES: A positive way my actions can affect others today.

POSITIVES: What went better than I expected today?

CHALLENGES: It was at this turning point today that I started to see progress.

KINDNESS: One kind & loving statement I can say to myself after a difficult day.

---

3. Wednesday

PRESENCE: Feeling into just this present moment, I notice.

_____

_____

_____

INTENTION: I will connect back into feeling the present moment during these kinds of stressful/busy times.

_____

_____

_____

RESOURCES: A negative belief or behaviour pattern I can observe & gently question today.

_____

_____

_____

POSITIVES: What positive outcome today made me feel supported or cared for?

_____

_____

_____

CHALLENGES: A wonderful way to recharge during or at the end of a challenging day.

_____

_____

_____

KINDNESS: To nurture more self-acceptance in my thoughts tomorrow I will.

_____

_____

4. Thursday

PRESENCE: The sensations I notice in my surroundings—temperature, texture, light.

_____

_____

_____

INTENTION: I can remain calm when I encounter these challenges today.

_____

_____

_____

RESOURCES: Today I can take small and gentle steps towards...

_____

_____

_____

POSITIVES: In what positive way did I handle stress or frustration today?

_____

_____

_____

CHALLENGES: A recent difficulty helped me discover this new strength within myself.

_____

_____

_____

KINDNESS: One negative thought I can let go of tonight, & and the positive I replace it with.

_____

_____

_____

5. Friday

PRESENCE: In this quiet moment of stillness, the thought that is challenging me is...

_____

_____

_____

INTENTION: When I observe this thoughts without attaching to it, it looks....
(colour/texture/temperature)

_____

_____

_____

RESOURCES: I can bring my resilience & power to these situations today.

_____

_____

_____

POSITIVES: A recent challenge that has helped me grow & that I now feel grateful for.

_____

_____

_____

CHALLENGES: What frustrated me the most about today, & how can I approach it differently next time?

_____

_____

_____

KINDNESS: How did I honour my feelings today, & how can I do that more often?

_____

_____

_____

6. Saturday

PRESENCE: Reflecting on the process of something I am doing, rather than the future outcome reminds me...

_____

_____

INTENTION: I can show myself love today by...

_____

_____

RESOURCES: I can plan to cultivate more peace in these aspects of my day today.

_____

_____

_____

POSITIVES: How did I make a positive impact on someone else's day today?

_____

_____

CHALLENGES: A creative solution I have found for a problem that I will use again.

_____

_____

KINDNESS: A kindness I have given to someone that I will give again.

_____

_____

7. Sunday

PRESENCE: When I imagine stepping back and observing my feelings flow this morning, I can describe it as...

___
___
___

INTENTION: At these times my productivity slows, & but my worth always stays the same.

___
___
___

RESOURCES: What I can offer myself to feel calm & okay, during moments of frustration.

___
___
___

POSITIVES: What experience today made me feel content or fulfilled?

___
___
___

CHALLENGES: How can I approach tomorrow with a growth mindset?

___
___
___

KINDNESS: I embrace these unique qualities in others, & in myself.

___
___
___

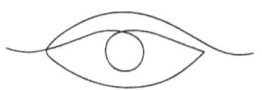

REFLECT
What did you learn from an interaction with someone new this week?

___

REFOCUS
How can you open yourself up to new connections or perspectives next week?

___

8. Monday

PRESENCE: When I use deep breathing to relax ; my body & mind feel...

_____

_____

INTENTION: My responsibilities today & my intended acts of self-care...

_____

_____

RESOURCES: My instincts are guiding me to....

_____

_____

_____

POSITIVES: Someone I supported or listened to today, & the the gratitude it gives me.

_____

_____

CHALLENGES: An optimistic account of the challenges I have ahead of me.

_____

_____

KINDNESS: A habit or practice I can build that will reinforce positive self-talk in my daily life.

_____

_____

_____

9. Tuesday

PRESENCE: A thought I am curious about.

___
___
___

INTENTION: I can nurture peace in my mind today by...

___
___
___

RESOURCES: A strength I can use to help others today.

___
___
___

POSITIVES: What was the best part of my day, & why did it stand out?

___
___
___

CHALLENGES: The first thought I had when faced with a challenge today, & how it shaped my response.

___
___
___

KINDNESS: A thought & an action from today that offered kindness to myself or others.

___
___
___

10. Wednesday

PRESENCE: Feeling present now feels... I will use this resource at these times/breaks/moments today.

___

___

___

INTENTION: Starting the day without putting unnecessary pressure on myself looks like...

___

___

___

RESOURCES: The actions I will take today to maintain my balance & calm.

___

___

___

POSITIVES: An experience today that opened my heart.

___

___

___

CHALLENGES: A fear or doubt, big or small, that I overcame today.

___

___

___

KINDNESS: Who I have shown compassion towards recently, how it felt, & when I can show myself the same.

___

___

___

11. Thursday

PRESENCE: When I bring attention to my breathing right now, I notice...

___

___

___

INTENTION: There is room in my day here... to offer myself this same kindness I would to a friend.

___

___

___

RESOURCES: I have felt confident when... and I can use this feeling to maintain my confidence today when...

___

___

___

POSITIVES: What did I learn today that I am grateful for?

___

___

CHALLENGES: When I am patient with myself during challenging moments I notice...

___

___

___

KINDNESS: What is one way I can share kindness with others tomorrow?

___

___

12. Friday

PRESENCE: An emotion I am noticing moving through me this morning is...

INTENTION: My worth feels valued when...

RESOURCES: I have noted these triggers... I have for this emotion... and I will soothe/calm myself mindfully through them by...

POSITIVES: A relationship I nurtured in a positive way today.

CHALLENGES: One way I successfully adapted to a situation today.

KINDNESS: One self-judgment I noticed today & the self-acceptance I can offer to replace it.

---

13. Saturday

PRESENCE: What small detail of this morning can I focus on to bring myself into this moment?

_____

_____

INTENTION: One way I can prioritise my mental & emotional health today.

_____

_____

RESOURCES: These priorities I have today... can be supported by these resources I have...

_____

_____

_____

POSITIVES: Something unexpected today that I am thankful for.

_____

_____

CHALLENGES: A challenge that has given me motivation to improve.

_____

_____

KINDNESS: Something kind I said/did for someone today...

_____

_____

_____

14. Sunday

PRESENCE: Being mindful of the natural world around me now, I feel....

___

INTENTION: When worry comes my way today, I can do this to detach from it & feel ok.

___

RESOURCES: These personal strengths... will support the decisions I make today.

___

POSITIVES: One positive outcome of my actions today.

___

CHALLENGES: A challenge today that I enjoyed and hope more of the same lie ahead.

___

KINDNESS: In moments of stress or anxiety, I will offer these kind words in self-talk, & to those around me.

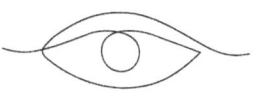

REFLECT
What is one thing you did this week to support your long-term goals?

___
___
___
___
___
___
___
___

REFOCUS
What's the next small step you can take toward achieving your goals next week?

___
___
___
___
___
___
___
___

15. Monday

PRESENCE: I can observe my attention on the now, pulling it back from future worries or past ruminations feels...

___
___
___

INTENTION: A task I can break down into smaller manageable steps today.

___
___
___

RESOURCES: In my day ahead, I will show myself compassion when...

___
___
___

POSITIVES: What kindness did someone show me today that I appreciate?

___
___
___

CHALLENGES: One way I can stay patient & calm when challenges arise.

___
___
___

KINDNESS: Someone I would like to check in on more regularly.

___
___
___

16. Tuesday

PRESENCE: I have noticed that bringing my attention to the present moment has these greater benefits for me.

___

INTENTION: An act of self love I can take today.

___

RESOURCES: Remaining centered in my strength today will allow me to be more open to....

___

POSITIVES: How did I express or receive love & care today?

___

CHALLENGES: A problem-solving technique that worked best for me today.

___

KINDNESS: One thing I want to tell myself tonight to reinforce my sense of worthiness.

___

17. Wednesday

PRESENCE: When I observe my inner world with curiosity instead of judgment, I notice...

_____

_____

_____

INTENTION: When I make mistakes today, I will offer this kindness to myself...

_____

_____

_____

RESOURCES: An area of my day I will navigate gracefully today.

_____

_____

_____

POSITIVES: One thing about my emotional or mental health that I feel grateful for today.

_____

_____

_____

CHALLENGES: A change I have embraced, even though it felt uncomfortable or difficult at first...

_____

_____

_____

KINDNESS: A flaw I've been hard on myself about, & a softened thought I offer now.

_____

_____

_____

18. Thursday

PRESENCE: Soft breath, deep breath, shallow breath: changing my breath, I notice...

INTENTION: What does a balanced, peaceful day look like for me today?

RESOURCES: What I can bring into my relationships & interactions today?

POSITIVES: A difficulty I am grateful I found the strength/courage to push through today.

CHALLENGES: How I can use that strength to approach tomorrow with more confidence.

KINDNESS: One practice I can use to cultivate more self-kindness in the days ahead.

---

19. Friday

PRESENCE: What does being present in conversations with others today look like & sound like?

_____

_____

INTENTION: A compassionate inner dialogue today starts with these words...

_____

_____

_____

RESOURCES: When self-compassion & self-confidence coexist it feels like...

_____

_____

_____

POSITIVES: What I feel the most thankful for today & how I can express that gratitude.

_____

_____

_____

CHALLENGES: A lesson I have learnt that will help me stay positive in the future.

_____

_____

_____

KINDNESS: Even when it's hard, I can speak kindly to myself. These are my fall back words of kindness...

_____

_____

_____

20. Saturday

PRESENCE: Finding stillness in my mind brings me...

INTENTION: To help me approach challenges calmly & with clarity today, I will...

RESOURCES: I acknowledge these personal strengths as I start my day.

POSITIVES: One small thing that I might normally overlook but feel grateful for.

CHALLENGES: The emotions that came up for me at challenging times today.

KINDNESS: One positive thing I can say to myself right now to show kindness.

---

21. Sunday

PRESENCE: As I move or stretch my body this morning, the sensations I notice are...

_____

_____

_____

INTENTION: In difficult moments today, I will offer myself compassion by...

_____

_____

RESOURCES: As I challenge myself today by... I will balance in self-care by...

_____

_____

_____

POSITIVES: How did I positively impact someone else's day today?

_____

_____

_____

CHALLENGES: A unique power I have discovered in myself.

_____

_____

_____

KINDNESS: A judgement I chose not to put on myself or someone else today.

_____

_____

_____

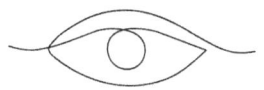

REFLECT
What part of your routine was most effective this week?

_____
_____
_____
_____
_____
_____
_____
_____
_____

REFOCUS
How can you streamline or improve your routine next week?

_____
_____
_____
_____
_____
_____
_____
_____
_____

22. Monday

PRESENCE: I notice today, emotionally I am feeling... I can support, move through or prepare for these feelings today by...

___

___

___

INTENTION: When I feel myself comparing myself to others today I will...

___

___

___

RESOURCES: Something unique about me that I will carry confidently into the day.

___

___

___

POSITIVES: One thing about my community that I am grateful for today.

___

___

___

CHALLENGES: My approach to this challenge showed me I am stronger than I thought.

___

___

___

KINDNESS: How can I support myself (and loved ones) with more love & care during challenging times?

___

___

___

23. Tuesday

PRESENCE: The words I have to describe being present this morning:

INTENTION: Staying within my personal boundaries today looks like...

RESOURCES: A mindful practice I can use today & when it will be useful.

POSITIVES: How I practiced patience or understanding today, & how it affected my interactions.

CHALLENGES: A mistake I have resolved with flexibility or problem-solving skills.

KINDNESS: A loving act toward myself (or someone else) I can give tomorrow.

---

24. Wednesday

PRESENCE: When I use my breath to anchor myself in the present moment it helps...

_____

_____

INTENTION: I can avoid rushing through my day & stay balanced by...

_____

_____

RESOURCES: I can visualise myself in ease & flow at this often challenging time of the day.

_____

_____

_____

POSITIVES: Something I relied on today that made my day easier.

_____

_____

CHALLENGES: A time I learnt to be brave in an uncertain situation.

_____

_____

KINDNESS: A mistake I have let go of and the lesson I have kept.

_____

_____

25. Thursday

PRESENCE: My description of a small, often unnoticed detail in my environment.

_____
_____
_____

INTENTION: When I feel my mind starting to overthink... I can tell myself...

_____
_____
_____

RESOURCES: I will use my compassion to support... (someone) through (something) today.

_____
_____
_____

POSITIVES: A small, comforting ritual or routine in my day that I am grateful for.

_____
_____
_____

CHALLENGES: The most empowering part of my day today.

_____
_____
_____

KINDNESS: What encouraging words can I use to support myself tomorrow?

_____
_____
_____

26. Friday

PRESENCE: A peaceful moment that quietens the mental noise today feels...

INTENTION: When I start to feel distracted today, I can gently refocus myself by...

RESOURCES: The best way to nurture productivity in my day today.

POSITIVES: The joy or creativity I am grateful for today.

CHALLENGES: The positive habits or practices that helped me reduce stress today.

KINDNESS: One thing I can do tomorrow to support my emotional self-care.

27. Saturday

PRESENCE: Breathing mindfully right now feels... & I can use this today when...

___

___

___

INTENTION: I can be kinder to myself when...

___

___

___

RESOURCES: One area of my day where I will try to balance being strong & being gentle with myself.

___

___

___

POSITIVES: Something comforting or reassuring about today that I am grateful for.

___

___

___

CHALLENGES: A moment when I got to practice thinking on my feet.

___

___

___

KINDNESS: Something I can do to make a positive difference to someone else tomorrow.

___

___

___

28. Sunday

PRESENCE: A common story I notice I am telling myself & the way I am rewriting it.

___

INTENTION: When self-doubt appears today I can release it by...

___

RESOURCES: A challenge coming for me today that I will use as a chance to grow...

___

POSITIVES: Someone or something that made me smile today.

___

CHALLENGES: Something I could & something I could not control today.

___

KINDNESS: When I'm feeling less than perfect, I can show kindness to myself by...

___

R & R

REFLECT
How did you honor your personal boundaries this week?

_____
_____
_____
_____
_____
_____
_____
_____

REFOCUS
What boundaries need reinforcing next week for your well-being?

_____
_____
_____
_____
_____
_____
_____
_____

29. Monday

PRESENCE: Savouring this moment... it looks, feels, sounds, tastes, smells like...

INTENTION: My day ahead in self-acceptance & peace could feel...

RESOURCES: I can make confident, aligned choices today when...

POSITIVES: A positive thought or attitude I want to carry with me into tomorrow.

CHALLENGES: One way I can practice positivity when facing a challenge.

KINDNESS: Did I notice my self-talk improving today, & what can I do to continue?

---

30. Tuesday

PRESENCE: What thoughts are taking up space in my mind, & how can I soften them?

___

INTENTION: What does a calm & peaceful day look like for me?

___

RESOURCES: When can I choose to feel strong today?

___

POSITIVES: A natural beauty or environment around me that I noticed today.

___

CHALLENGES: A learning experience I had today.

___

KINDNESS: How can I be more loving toward myself when things are difficult?

___

Right and Left Breathing:

For balance, heart & lung health, stress release, & memory health.

Start with your right index and middle fingers pointing up between the eyebrows - bend the ring and pinky fingers down and rest them outside the left nostril, have the thumb in place resting at the right nostril.

1. Exhale out of both nostrils
2. Use the thumb to close the right nostril and breathe in through the left
3. Release the thumb and close the left nostril with the ring finger & pinky
4. Exhale through the right nostril.
5. Pause and then inhale again through the right.
6. Pause and release the ring finger. Close the right again with the thumb.
7. Exhale, pause, inhale with the left.
8. return to step 3 and continue the cycle for 2-3 minutes or as long as feels comfortable.

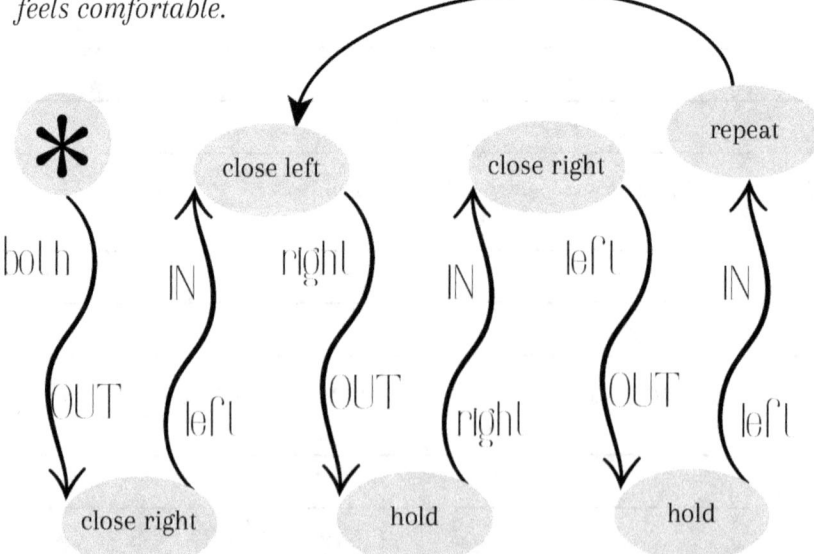

**Please use this technique mindfully & stop if you are feeling strain, overwhelm or find the practice triggering for you.

October

Embracing Balance and Harmony

As spring turns toward summer, visualise a life of balance & harmony. Picture yourself walking a path that balances your personal, professional, & emotional needs. What areas of your life need more balance? Consider your health, career, relationships, personal growth...

See yourself making mindful adjustments, whether it's setting boundaries, prioritizing rest, or focusing on relationships. Imagine how achieving this balance allows you to feel more at peace, fulfilled, & in control of your time & energy.

1. Wednesday

PRESENCE: Tuning in to my body, I notice it needs... today.

_____

_____

_____

INTENTION: Some learning I intend to gather through my day today.

_____

_____

RESOURCES: How can I be my own best supporter today?

_____

_____

_____

POSITIVES: A small, joyful moment I experienced today.

_____

_____

_____

CHALLENGES: What future challenges do I look forward to embracing?

_____

_____

_____

KINDNESS: My imperfections are perfect for me in this way...

_____

_____

_____

2. Thursday

PRESENCE: Am I noticing any uncomfortable emotions, & can I simply observe them?

___

INTENTION: If I have any moments of doubt today, I offer this mantra of self-acceptance.

___

RESOURCES: At these choice points today I can let my self-awareness inform my decisions & behaviours.

___

POSITIVES: What freedom or choice today am I thankful for?

___

CHALLENGES: What mindset helped me push through the toughest part of today?

___

KINDNESS: What is one way I can transform self-criticism into self-encouragement tomorrow?

3. Friday

PRESENCE: How can I invite a sense of stillness & mindfulness into this day?

___

___

INTENTION: I will respect my own energy levels during these times today.

___

___

RESOURCES: Observing my inner dialogue today, I can shift it in this empowering direction...

___

___

___

POSITIVES: What positive changes have I noticed in myself over this time?

___

___

CHALLENGES: What lessons learned from today can I embrace & apply tomorrow?

___

___

KINDNESS: How can I be more patient & accepting of my personal journey & growth?

___

___

___

4. Saturday

PRESENCE: Often the space around me reflects the way I feel, so how can I use this knowledge to support myself?

INTENTION: I can make space for joy & self-acceptance in these ways today.

RESOURCES: I can use both strength & mindfulness to face this challenge today.

POSITIVES: What made my day feel easier or more manageable?

CHALLENGES: One way I can release any remaining stress from today before I go to bed.

KINDNESS: One way I can make speaking kindly to myself a daily habit.

---

5. Sunday

PRESENCE: What thoughts are present for me this morning?

_____

_____

INTENTION: How could I remain calm in my mind today?

_____

_____

RESOURCES: Which of my personal strengths could be my focus today?

_____

_____

POSITIVES: What was a moment today that made me feel proud of myself?

_____

_____

CHALLENGES: How did I initially respond to the biggest challenge of my day?

_____

_____

KINDNESS: What is one kind thing I did for myself today?

_____

_____

_____

R & R

REFLECT
What's one area of your life where you noticed progress this week?

_____
_____
_____
_____
_____
_____
_____
_____

REFOCUS
What can you do to keep the momentum going in that area next week?

_____
_____
_____
_____
_____
_____
_____
_____

6. Monday

PRESENCE: What distractions are pulling me away from the present moment right now, & how can I let them go?

_____

_____

_____

INTENTION: In what ways can I practice patience with myself today?

_____

_____

_____

RESOURCES: How can I balance my desire for growth with the need to be kind to myself today?

_____

_____

_____

POSITIVES: What is something I did today that I feel proud & thankful for?

_____

_____

_____

CHALLENGES: What strength did I rely on to get through challenges today?

_____

_____

_____

KINDNESS: How did I take care of my emotional well-being today, & how can I continue to do so?

_____

_____

_____

7. Tuesday

PRESENCE: How can I approach my tasks today with more presence & awareness?

___
___
___

INTENTION: How can I show myself love & care today?

___
___
___

RESOURCES: How can I maintain a sense of inner calm today, while also leaning into my strengths?

___
___
___

POSITIVES: How did I feel connected to others in a meaningful way today?

___
___
___

CHALLENGES: A challenge today allow me to practice my problem-solving skills.

___
___
___

KINDNESS: What did I do today that made me feel proud of myself?

___
___
___

8. Wednesday

PRESENCE: With eyes closed, my inner mind feels...

INTENTION: Where in my day can I quiet the inner critic & trust myself more?

RESOURCES: How can I respond to challenges today with more awareness & mindfulness?

POSITIVES: What is one thing about my life today that brings me peace or comfort?

CHALLENGES: How were my challenges important to my personal growth?

KINDNESS: How can I show kindness to myself when I make a mistake?

---

9. Thursday

PRESENCE: Focusing on the rhythm of my breath, how does it feel?

___

___

___

INTENTION: What can I do today to feel more balanced & centred?

___

___

___

RESOURCES: How can I use my self awareness to approach today with more clarity?

___

___

___

POSITIVES: What is one thing I accomplished today, big or small, that I am proud of?

___

___

___

CHALLENGES: What obstacles today helped me build confidence in my abilities?

___

___

___

KINDNESS: The self-compassion of today that I will carry into tomorrow.

___

___

___

10. Friday

PRESENCE: Sitting with the here & now, the sensations I observe are...

_____
_____
_____

INTENTION: What supports can I use to enter this day with an open heart & mind?

_____
_____
_____

RESOURCES: What growth am I experiencing, & how can I nurture it?

_____
_____
_____

POSITIVES: What am I most grateful for today, & why does it matter to me?

_____
_____
_____

CHALLENGES: How can I end the day feeling positive about the challenges I faced?

_____
_____
_____

KINDNESS: How did I improve my self-talk today, & what can I do to keep progressing?

_____
_____
_____

11. Saturday

PRESENCE: Observing my thoughts without judgement feels like...

INTENTION: One thing I can do to stay calm during stressful moments today is...

RESOURCES: How can I build on the resilience I have shown?

POSITIVES: What is one interaction or conversation that had a positive impact on me today?

CHALLENGES: How did today's challenges make me feel, & why?

KINDNESS: In what ways can I be gentler with myself in moments of frustration?

12. Sunday

PRESENCE: As I scan my body this morning I notice it feels...

_____
_____
_____

INTENTION: What does it look like to forgive myself today, if things don't go as planned?

_____
_____
_____

RESOURCES: How can I move forward today with confidence in my abilities?

_____
_____
_____

POSITIVES: What is something I own that I felt grateful to have today?

_____
_____
_____

CHALLENGES: What positive outcomes could come from the challenges of today?

_____
_____
_____

KINDNESS: A self-critical thought I had today, & it's replacement in self-compassion.

_____
_____
_____

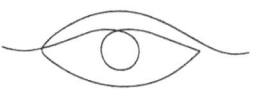

REFLECT
How did you manage your stress, worry or anxiety this week?

REFOCUS
What coping strategies or tools can you use next week for stress relief?

13. Monday

PRESENCE: What emotions can I observe, without getting caught up in them?

___

INTENTION: What would self-acceptance feel like as I move through today?

___

RESOURCES: Today I will observe with curiosity my response to these challenges...

___

POSITIVES: How did I practice kindness toward myself today?

___

CHALLENGES: How was I pushed outside my comfort zone, & what did I learn?

___

KINDNESS: When can I practice more positive self-talk when I feel self-critical?

___

14. Tuesday

PRESENCE: I can ground myself before beginning the tasks of the day by...

INTENTION: One boundary I can set today to protect my peace is...

RESOURCES: A choice I can make today to support balance for my mind &/or body.

POSITIVES: What is one skill or ability I used today that I am thankful for?

CHALLENGES: A setback I faced today that I can turn into a lesson for the future.

KINDNESS: What is one part of myself that I want to embrace with more acceptance?

---

15. Wednesday

PRESENCE: My observations of the sights & sounds surrounding me.

_____

_____

_____

INTENTION: One small thing I can let go of today that is causing me stress?

_____

_____

RESOURCES: One way I can acknowledge my strengths today (without needing validation from others)?

_____

_____

_____

POSITIVES: What did I do today to strengthen a relationship, & how did it feel?

_____

_____

_____

CHALLENGES: How did I demonstrate resilience today?

_____

_____

_____

KINDNESS: I can replace this negative thought with this uplifting one tomorrow.

_____

_____

_____

16. Thursday

PRESENCE: A calm space in my mind feels like...

_____

_____

_____

INTENTION: One way I can embrace the flow of the day without rushing through it...

_____

_____

_____

RESOURCES: I can enjoy growth today without pushing myself too hard by...

_____

_____

_____

POSITIVES: Who helped me feel more positive or supported today?

_____

_____

_____

CHALLENGES: How can I improve the way I handle frustration when facing difficulties?

_____

_____

_____

KINDNESS: Tomorrow I can show more emotional care toward myself by...

_____

_____

_____

17. Friday

PRESENCE: Focusing fully on each task without distraction today will feel...

_____
_____
_____

INTENTION: I will celebrate my uniqueness & individuality today by...

_____
_____
_____

RESOURCES: Balancing my strength & inner peace today looks like...

_____
_____
_____

POSITIVES: Which challenging situation positively impacted my day?

_____
_____
_____

CHALLENGES: What creative solutions did I come up with today?

_____
_____
_____

KINDNESS: I can remind myself of my worth, even when I am deeply challenged by...

_____
_____
_____

18. Saturday

PRESENCE: One inner feeling or sensation I observe this morning...

___
___
___

INTENTION: Where in my day can I see room to be less hard on myself?

___
___
___

RESOURCES: At these times today... I can remind myself that I have everything I need within me to navigate challenges.

___
___
___

POSITIVES: What is one way in which today's events unfolded that I am thankful for?

___
___
___

CHALLENGES: What did today's difficulty teach me about adapting to change?

___
___
___

KINDNESS: What imperfection did I notice in myself today, & how can I embrace it with love?

___
___
___

19. Sunday

PRESENCE: How it feels to take a deep, mindful breath & pause right now.

___

INTENTION: I can maintain a balance between work & rest today by...

___

RESOURCES: What do I know about myself that will support my tasks & interactions today?

___

POSITIVES: How did I stay focused & productive today, & what made that possible?

___

CHALLENGES: What have I learnt about stepping into discomfort with courage?

___

KINDNESS: What is one thing I can let go of tonight in order to show myself more kindness tomorrow?

___

R & R

REFLECT
Which of your passions or hobbies did you make time for this week?

_____
_____
_____
_____
_____
_____
_____
_____

REFOCUS
How can you make more space for activities that bring you joy next week?

_____
_____
_____
_____
_____
_____
_____
_____

20. Monday

PRESENCE: What does it feel like to breathe in this moment & release the need to plan or worry about the rest of the day?

___

___

INTENTION: What does self-compassion look like for me as I start this day?

___

___

RESOURCES: I can remind myself that growth often comes from stepping outside of my comfort zone when...

___

___

___

POSITIVES: Who made me feel valued today, & why am I grateful for it?

___

___

CHALLENGES: One positive from today's challenge that I want to remember...

___

___

KINDNESS: A self-critical thought I'd like to challenge & replace with a positive one.

___

___

___

21. Tuesday

PRESENCE: What is my mind focusing on at this moment, & how does it affect me?

_____
_____
_____

INTENTION: A kind & compassionate thought I can use for myself today.

_____
_____
_____

RESOURCES: One way I can rely on my inner strength to navigate challenges today:

_____
_____
_____

POSITIVES: What is one thing today that I am truly grateful for?

_____
_____
_____

CHALLENGES: The hardest part of today, & what I learnt about myself from facing it.

_____
_____
_____

KINDNESS: One kind thought I want to tell myself before bed tonight.

_____
_____
_____

22. Wednesday

PRESENCE: Listening closely to the signals my body is sending me, I notice...

INTENTION: Where in my day can I offer compassion to myself?

RESOURCES: One area where I'd like to deepen my self-awareness today...

POSITIVES: What positive habit did I follow through with today, & how did it make me feel?

CHALLENGES: What did I gain from the challenges today that I didn't expect?

KINDNESS: What I forgive myself for today (no matter how small).

23. Thursday

PRESENCE: I gently check in with my emotions and feel...

INTENTION: When can I remind myself that I am enough, exactly as I am today?

RESOURCES: What is one challenge I can face with strength & self-compassion today?

POSITIVES: What is something about my home that I appreciate today?

CHALLENGES: One small win I experienced today.

KINDNESS: How did I practice self-acceptance today, & what did it feel like?

---

24. Friday

PRESENCE: The temperature of my breath this morning feels...

INTENTION: I can stay in tune with my emotional needs today by...

RESOURCES: Today I can focus on aligning with this personal value of mine.

POSITIVES: How did I balance productivity & rest today in a way that felt good?

CHALLENGES: What can I improve on the next time I encounter a challenge like the one I had today?

KINDNESS: An affirming statement I can tell myself to reinforce my self-worth.

25. Saturday

PRESENCE: The things I see, hear, feel, touch, taste in the world around me this day.

INTENTION: I describe this plan to take a break if I feel overwhelmed today.

RESOURCES: How I can stay true to myself, when faced with opposition or difficulty today.

POSITIVES: Who made my day easier or more enjoyable, & how can I show them gratitude?

CHALLENGES: How can I build on the flexibility I have shown when faced with a challenge?

KINDNESS: I can be more patient with myself when I'm feeling overwhelmed by...

---

26. Sunday

PRESENCE: One thought or concern I can set aside to focus on the present is...

_____
_____

INTENTION: What does it look like to stay present today?

_____
_____

RESOURCES: How can I pace my day productively & avoid feeling rushed?

_____
_____

POSITIVES: How did I respond to a situation today that showed growth in my mindset or behaviour?

_____
_____

CHALLENGES: What have I learnt about staying calm & centred during stressful moments?

_____
_____

KINDNESS: What is one way I can boost my sense of self-worth tomorrow?

_____
_____

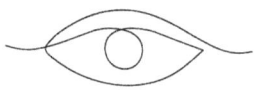

REFLECT
What's one thing you're grateful for this week, & why?

_____
_____
_____
_____
_____
_____
_____
_____
_____

REFOCUS
How can you cultivate more moments of gratitude in the coming week?

_____
_____
_____
_____
_____
_____
_____
_____

27. Monday

PRESENCE: Feeling into the soles of my feet this morning, I notice...?

INTENTION: One thing I can do to prioritise my well-being today.

RESOURCES: How can I use my strength to create more peace & harmony in my day?

POSITIVES: Who am I thankful for being in my life today, & why?

CHALLENGES: A creative response I have had to a challenging situation.

KINDNESS: I am learning to be compassionate toward these beautiful flaws & imperfections.

---

28. Tuesday

PRESENCE: When I feel my mind is wandering, I gently bring it back to the present by...

___

___

___

INTENTION: I can remind myself that I am are worthy of kindness & understanding with these words...

___

___

___

RESOURCES: How can I respond, rather than react, to difficulties today?

___

___

___

POSITIVES: What is one way I made time for self-care today, & how did it enhance my mood?

___

___

___

CHALLENGES: How did I adapt in the day, & what did I learn from adapting?

___

___

___

KINDNESS: I can offer myself more compassion tomorrow by...

___

___

29. Wednesday

PRESENCE: When I breathe deeply & consciously I notice...

INTENTION: How can I create more peace in my day today?

RESOURCES: How can I use what I know of my self to improve this day?

POSITIVES: What is one accomplishment from today that I am grateful for?

CHALLENGES: The confidence I gained today, & how I will carry it into future challenges?

KINDNESS: One affirmation I can repeat to myself tomorrow to encourage positive self-talk.

30. Thursday

PRESENCE: Focusing on the sound of my breath, I notice...

INTENTION: One way I can approach today with ease & self-kindness.

RESOURCES: I can act with both confidence & compassion towards myself & others today when...

POSITIVES: What positive feelings am I taking with me into tomorrow?

CHALLENGES: Rather than these setbacks, I can focus on this progress I made today.

KINDNESS: What is one thing I can forgive myself for today?

31. Friday

PRESENCE: I gently redirect to the present moment when my mind wanders & notice...

INTENTION: What would it feel like to go through the day with a peaceful mindset?

RESOURCES: I can remind myself of my strengths when faced with these kinds of difficulties today.

POSITIVES: Which person am I thankful for today, & why?

CHALLENGES: Which challenge offered me an opportunity for growth today?

KINDNESS: How did I take care of my emotional well-being today?

November

Expanding Your Vision

As the energy of summer builds, visualise yourself expanding into new horizons. Picture yourself standing at the top of a mountain, with a clear view of your life's path ahead. What bold steps can you take this month to move closer to your dreams? See yourself embracing new opportunities, overcoming any fears or doubts, and taking inspired action. Imagine how expanding your vision leads to exciting growth & a deeper sense of purpose.

Change in the night:

Encourage the mind to shift focus from worry to calm, & prepare for a deeper sleep.

1. Close your eyes & bring to mind a worry that is blocking you from sleep.

2. Notice the sensory qualities of this worry:
   - Is it a clear image, a feeling, or a sound?
   - How big or small is the image or feeling?
   - Notice it's brightness & volume - bright, dim, loud or soft?
   - Is it close to you, or further away?
   - What colour/s are there - or is it black & white?
   - Is it still, or does it move?
   - Does it have a temperature or a texture?

3. Adjusting these qualities:
   - **Shrink it**: If your worry feels large & overpowering, imagine it shrinking in size until it's small & manageable.
   - **Dim and Dull it**: Lower the brightness of the image or feeling until it's barely visible, like a distant shape in the fog.
   - **Move it Far Away**: Imagine pushing the image or sound away from you, placing it at a comfortable distance until it feels less intense.
   - **Change it:** Give it a different colour, or take all colour away, alter the temperature, texture & weight.

4. Surround the worry in a calm or soft colour.

5. Fade or dissolve the worry: imagine it gradually disappearing like a fog getting thinner & thinner as the sun dissipates it. Notice how you are feeling - lighter? more relaxed? distanced from the worry?

6. Replace it with a calming thought or image: bring a thought in that makes you feel relaxed & safe: a beach, a holiday, a gentle memory.

7. Give this thought quality: make it warm, bright, close & comforting.

1. Saturday

PRESENCE: What is my body asking for right now—rest, movement, nourishment, or something else?

_____
_____
_____

INTENTION: Responding to mistakes with patience today, looks like...

_____
_____
_____

RESOURCES: How I want to feel at the end of today, & how I can encourage it?

_____
_____
_____

POSITIVES: What made me smile or laugh today,?

_____
_____
_____

CHALLENGES: How could today's challenge be preparing me for future situations?

_____
_____
_____

KINDNESS: My struggles & imperfections, and the understanding I offer them.

_____
_____
_____

2. Sunday

PRESENCE: Checking in with my emotions, I notice I feel...

_____

_____

INTENTION: What would it look like to accept my emotions today, even the uncomfortable ones?

_____

_____

RESOURCES: I can check on my thoughts & feelings during these situations today...

_____

_____

POSITIVES: What is one piece of good news or positivity that came my way today?

_____

_____

CHALLENGES: How did I stay grounded when dealing with difficulty today?

_____

_____

KINDNESS: Tomorrow I can remind myself that it's okay to be imperfect by...

_____

_____

R & R

REFLECT
How did you prioritize your mental or emotional health this week?

_____
_____
_____
_____
_____
_____
_____
_____

REFOCUS
What will you do next week to continue nurturing your mental & emotional well-being?

_____
_____
_____
_____
_____
_____
_____
_____

3. Monday

PRESENCE: When I deepen my breath into my belly, I feel...

INTENTION: I can communicate my needs to others clearly today when...

RESOURCES: I can reflect my values through these actions today...

POSITIVES: What made me feel connected to others today?

CHALLENGES: In a difficult situation I can be compassionate toward myself by...

KINDNESS: The best way I can remind myself that I am enough, just as I am.

4. Tuesday

PRESENCE: One thing I can notice in my environment that I've not paid attention to before...

___
___
___

INTENTION: I can remain grounded in the face of stress today by...

___
___
___

RESOURCES: Some actions I can take today to reflect my strength & resolve are...

___
___
___

POSITIVES: What is something today that reminded me of the goodness in life?

___
___
___

CHALLENGES: What resources did I use today to help me stay strong during challenges?

___
___
___

KINDNESS: When things don't go as planned, I can remind myself of these kind words.

___
___
___

5. Wednesday

PRESENCE: When I close my eyes & release the clutter in my mind it looks...

INTENTION: In which spaces can I remind myself to pause & breathe today?

RESOURCES: I can navigate the priorities today with a sense of ease by...

POSITIVES: One thing that went smoothly or easily for me today.

CHALLENGES: What positive coping mechanisms do I have for stressful challenges?

KINDNESS: What emotion did I allow myself to feel fully today, without judgment?

---

6. Thursday

PRESENCE: While eating breakfast slowly & mindfully, I notice...

INTENTION: I can nurture my emotions today by...

RESOURCES: In what situations can I use inner calm to anchor my strength today?

POSITIVES: What resource or opportunity was I grateful for today?

CHALLENGES: How have my critical thinking skills helped with a challenge?

KINDNESS: My worth extends beyond my achievements or productivity. I know I have these positive qualities.

---

7. Friday

PRESENCE: Is there a thought pattern I am noticing that I can choose not to engage with today?

_____

_____

_____

INTENTION: One thing I can do to create balance in my relationships today is...

_____

_____

RESOURCES: In today's potential challenges, I will use this mindful approach...

_____

_____

_____

POSITIVES: What friendship am I grateful for, & why?

_____

_____

CHALLENGES: An experience I've had that has taught me a better version of myself.

_____

_____

KINDNESS: Which area of my life needs more self-compassion practice?

_____

_____

_____

8. Saturday

PRESENCE: The movement of my breath today feels...

___
___
___

INTENTION: What does loving my imperfections look sound like today?

___
___
___

RESOURCES: When I act in alignment with my values it feels...

___
___
___

POSITIVES: What is one resource or tool that helped me succeed today?

___
___
___

CHALLENGES: When have I trusted myself through a decision or challenge, & how did it feel?

___
___
___

KINDNESS: What can I do tomorrow to continue practicing self-kindness in difficult moments?

___
___
___

9. Sunday

PRESENCE: Feeling present and releasing worry about the future feels...

INTENTION: One way I can respond to myself with empathy today...

RESOURCES: When I trust in myself, decisions today look...

POSITIVES: Where did I respond with positivity or strength today?

CHALLENGES: What lessons from today can I use to create a better tomorrow?

KINDNESS: Where can I put more loving & supportive self-talk into my daily routine?

R & R

REFLECT
How did you feel most supported by others this week?

REFOCUS
How can you give or receive support more openly next week?

10. Monday

PRESENCE: When I close my eyes and breathe kindly, I see...

___
___
___

INTENTION: Where/when can I slow down & enjoy the present moment today?

___
___

RESOURCES: One challenge I have overcome that proves my ability to grow is...

___
___
___

POSITIVES: What opportunity or experience today am I most thankful for?

___
___

CHALLENGES: What did today reveal about my strengths or weaknesses?

___
___

KINDNESS: One small act of self-kindness I can do for myself tomorrow.

___
___

II. Tuesday

PRESENCE: This morning my energy levels in my body are...

INTENTION: I can remember to speak to myself kindly today when...

RESOURCES: What small step toward growth can I take today, even if it feels uncomfortable?

POSITIVES: What was the most peaceful or calming moment of my day?

CHALLENGES: The challenges & valuable learning experiences I had today...

KINDNESS: When did I show myself compassion, & how did it feel?

---

12. Wednesday

PRESENCE: What emotions am I noticing this morning?

INTENTION: In what ways can I let go of the need to be perfect today?

RESOURCES: I can check in with my needs & emotions today by...

POSITIVES: What is one strength or skill I used today that I am thankful for?

CHALLENGES: What strategy worked well for me in harder moments today?

KINDNESS: I challenged this negative thought with this positive self-talk replacement.

13. Thursday

PRESENCE: When I observe the sensations in my relaxed hands, I notice...

INTENTION: One thing I can say "no" to today for my own well-being.

RESOURCES: I know myself well enough to know that today I will need this resource.

POSITIVES: One thing I learned today that will help me grow in a positive direction.

CHALLENGES: One thing I would do differently if I could redo a challenge in my day.

KINDNESS: One thing I did today that I completely accept without judgment.

---

14. Friday

PRESENCE: Right now, in my surroundings I am noticing...

INTENTION: One way I can make things easier for myself today.

RESOURCES: I can see myself pause & reflect before reacting to these kinds of difficult situations today...

POSITIVES: What positive memory from today do I want to cherish?

CHALLENGES: I can celebrate the strength I showed at difficult times today by...

KINDNESS: What is one positive affirmation I want to focus on for tomorrow?

15. Saturday

PRESENCE: When I still my mind, I find I can let go of this worry easily:

INTENTION: I can notice my reactions today with compassion and soothe myself by...

RESOURCES: One boundary I can assert in a kind, yet firm, way today.

POSITIVES: One positive decision I made today that I want to continue making.

CHALLENGES: What self-care practices could have helped me during stressful times today?

KINDNESS: How can I show myself more kindness when I'm feeling emotionally vulnerable?

16. Sunday

PRESENCE: When I am fully present for my morning cuppa today, I notice...

_____

_____

_____

INTENTION: One way I can honour my body & its needs today.

_____

_____

_____

RESOURCES: When difficulty shows up today, I will remain peaceful & strong by...

_____

_____

_____

POSITIVES: What is one thing I often take for granted that I felt thankful for today?

_____

_____

_____

CHALLENGES: Today encouraged me to find this new way to approach a problem.

_____

_____

_____

KINDNESS: The positive qualities I see in myself today, & how I can celebrate them.

_____

_____

_____

R & R

REFLECT
What did you discover about yourself through this week's experiences?

_____
_____
_____
_____
_____
_____
_____
_____
_____

REFOCUS
How can you use that self-discovery to approach next week with intention?

_____
_____
_____
_____
_____
_____
_____
_____
_____

17. Monday

PRESENCE: When I am patient and curious about my present thoughts, I notice...

_____

_____

INTENTION: When I notice negative self-talk today, I will...

_____

_____

RESOURCES: One way I can be kind to myself today.

_____

_____

POSITIVES: What is one thing I did to protect my energy or maintain balance today?

_____

_____

CHALLENGES: One way I may have grown through a situation/challenge today.

_____

_____

KINDNESS: The mistakes I made today, & why they are okay.

_____

_____

_____

18. Tuesday

PRESENCE: Focusing on my breath, I notice...

_____

_____

_____

INTENTION: Where can I cultivate more harmony in my environment today?

_____

_____

_____

RESOURCES: When I remain calm in the choices I make today, I feel...

_____

_____

_____

POSITIVES: What positive feedback or recognition did I receive today?

_____

_____

_____

CHALLENGES: These successes I choose to remember when I face future difficulties.

_____

_____

_____

KINDNESS: What unrealistic expectation of myself can I lift from my day tomorrow...

_____

_____

_____

19. Wednesday

PRESENCE: When I relax my mind & calm my thoughts it feels...

INTENTION: The qualities I have that I will let myself feel guided by today are...

RESOURCES: I can find confidence to approach these tasks today.

POSITIVES: What is one action I want to repeat because of its positive impact?

CHALLENGES: A challenge that passed me today & the learning I will keep from it.

KINDNESS: As I improve how I speak to myself - I hear myself saying...

/ 20. Thursday

PRESENCE: This morning my heart/soul feels...

INTENTION: How I can bring more calm into my interactions today.

RESOURCES: As I am noticing my power, things feel...

POSITIVES: How did I step outside of my comfort zone in a positive way today?

CHALLENGES: What challenge have I overcome that boosted my confidence?

KINDNESS: When I'm feeling overwhelmed, I will offer myself these kind words...

21. Friday

PRESENCE: What part of my body feels the most relaxed, & what part feels tense?

INTENTION: One way I can show myself understanding today.

RESOURCES: One way I can challenge myself today towards my goals.

POSITIVES: Who supported or helped me today, & how can I show gratitude?

CHALLENGES: One thing I could have done differently to make today easier on me.

KINDNESS: When I'm struggling, I will remind myself...

22. Saturday

PRESENCE: A feeling I am moving through, & how I will gently support myself.

INTENTION: Something I would like to improve on or learn today.

RESOURCES: Where/when can I take my time & respond more thoughtfully today?

POSITIVES: What interaction had a positive affect on my day?

CHALLENGES: Overcoming a challenge makes me feel...

KINDNESS: How did I move away from self-doubt & show myself love today?

---

23. Sunday

PRESENCE: When I slow down & savour the sensations of this moment, it feels...

INTENTION: In what way will I listen and respond to my body's needs today?

RESOURCES: What actions can I take today that align with my values & intentions?

POSITIVES: What am I most grateful for about the timing of events in my day?

CHALLENGES: The mistakes I made & what I learnt from them.

KINDNESS: How I can accept & celebrate my efforts of the day.

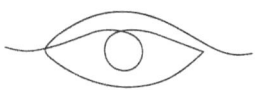

R & R

REFLECT
How did you create balance between work & personal time this week?

_____
_____
_____
_____
_____
_____
_____
_____

REFOCUS
What adjustments can you make to better balance your responsibilities next week?

_____
_____
_____
_____
_____
_____
_____
_____

24. Monday

PRESENCE: How the space I am in affects my mood, & what I notice about it right now.

___

___

___

INTENTION: One way I can release any tension in my body today.

___

___

RESOURCES: In situations that would typically cause stress today, I remain calm & strong by...

___

___

___

POSITIVES: The positive emotion I experienced the most today, & what created it.

___

___

CHALLENGES: A challenge that taught me about my ability to persevere recently.

___

___

KINDNESS: The kind words that uplifted me today, & where I will use them again.

___

___

___

25. Tuesday

PRESENCE: What is happening around me in this moment now?

INTENTION: One way I can be fully present in my tasks today.

RESOURCES: An area where I can gently push myself out of my comfort zone today.

POSITIVES: What is one thing about my environment today that I felt grateful for?

CHALLENGES: In what ways have I shown I can handle stress better than I thought?

KINDNESS: Tomorrow, I can nurture my emotional needs with compassion by...

---

26. Wednesday

PRESENCE: 5 slow, deep, belly breaths make me feel...

___
___
___

INTENTION: Who will I practice present & open communication with today?

___
___
___

RESOURCES: I will tune into my self-talk during these vulnerable spaces today... & offer these supportive words instead...

___
___
___

POSITIVES: How did I contribute positively to the people/group around me today?

___
___
___

CHALLENGES: An unexpected solution I found during a challenge.

___
___
___

KINDNESS: Did I acknowledge my self-worth today, & how can I ensure I do so tomorrow?

___
___
___

＃ 27. Thursday

PRESENCE: The thoughts I am having right now are... without judgement.

INTENTION: I can remind myself that I am doing the best I can today, when...

RESOURCES: It will be useful to stay present & centered when I am facing/doing this today.

POSITIVES: What positive surprise did today bring that I am grateful for?

CHALLENGES: I adapted when this happened today.

KINDNESS: An imperfection/mistake I can reframe with kindness.

---

28. Friday

PRESENCE: Taking a few moments of stillness to connect with my breath feels...

INTENTION: Today I can maintain a calm & balanced attitude when...

RESOURCES: At these difficult times today, I can focus on this growth it offers me.

POSITIVES: One way I maintained motivation throughout the day...

CHALLENGES: A moment that showed me I am capable of more than I thought...

KINDNESS: What is one thing I can tell myself tonight to ease any worries or self-doubt?

29. Saturday

PRESENCE: Letting the past be passed & focusing on right now, I notice...

INTENTION: At these times... I will choose to be gentle with myself by...

RESOURCES: I will choose self-confidence & self-belief today when...

POSITIVES: One inspiring thing I noticed today.

CHALLENGES: A positive mindset shift I have noticed in myself.

KINDNESS: A kindness I gave to someone today.

---

30. Sunday

PRESENCE: A thought pattern I am observing myself have.

_____

_____

_____

INTENTION: I can encourage a calm environment in my home/workspace today by...

_____

_____

_____

RESOURCES: I choose to stand confidently in my strengths today when...

_____

_____

_____

POSITIVES: What positive outcome or solution did I find today that made me feel good?

_____

_____

_____

CHALLENGES: A resource or support I use to handle challenging moments.

_____

_____

_____

KINDNESS: Something I did today that deserves self-praise or acknowledgment?

_____

_____

_____

R & R

REFLECT
What was the most rewarding part of this week, & how did it make you feel?

_____
_____
_____
_____
_____
_____
_____
_____

REFOCUS
What reward can you work toward in the upcoming week to stay motivated?

_____
_____
_____
_____
_____
_____
_____
_____

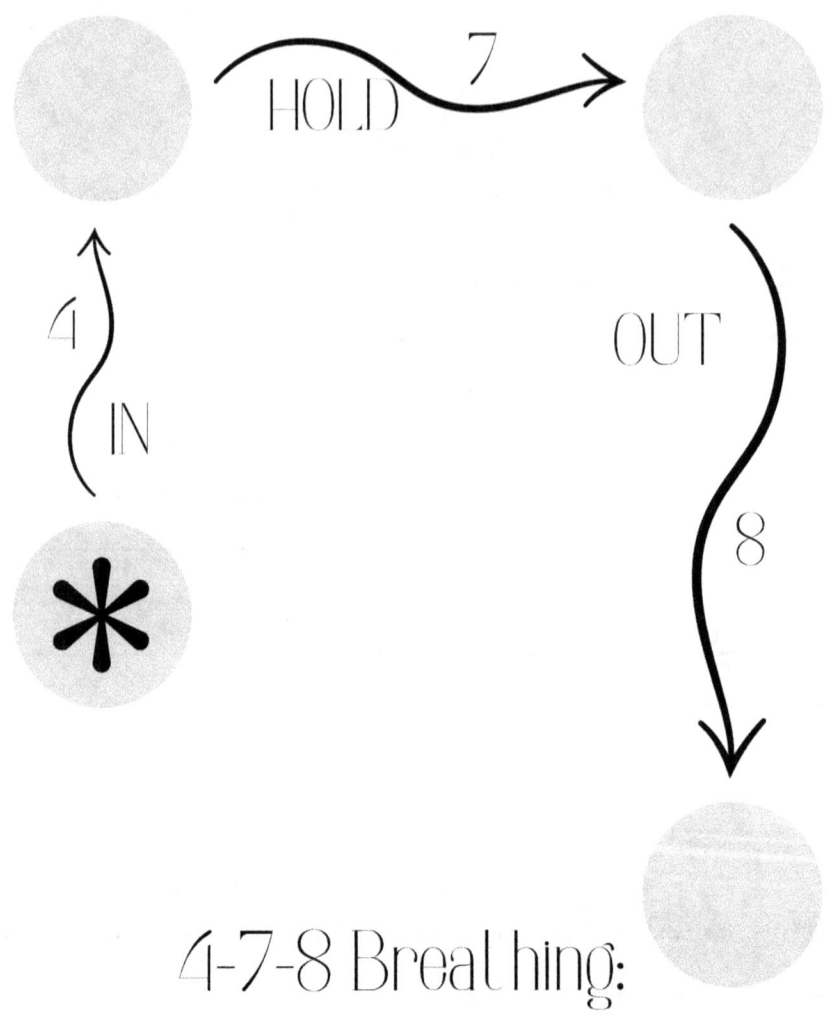

4-7-8 Breathing:

Activate a relaxation response and feel your tension breathe out & away.

Starting at the ✶. *Trace the arrows with your pointer finger.*
Change direction on the dots.
Inhale for the count of 4.
Hold for the count of 7.
Exhale for a count of 8.
Continue for 4 cycles, and work up to 8.

*Please use this technique mindfully & stop if you are feeling strain, overwhelm or find the practice triggering for you.

December

Reflection and Integration

As the year comes to a close and the festive season begins, visualise a kind reflecting on the year's journey. Picture a timeline of the year, highlighting moments of growth, challenges, & joy. How have you evolved? What lessons have you learned? See yourself integrating these experiences into a stronger, wiser version of yourself. Imagine feeling proud of the progress you've made, while also looking forward to the new year with optimism and clarity.

1. Monday

PRESENCE: Staying connected to my body as I move through today will feel...

_____

_____

INTENTION: I can ease up on self-criticism today when...

_____

_____

RESOURCES: To welcome & be open to new opportunities today I will...

_____

_____

_____

POSITIVES: A simple pleasure, (e.g. favorite meal or activity) I am grateful for today.

_____

_____

CHALLENGES: This challenge helped me grow today...

_____

_____

KINDNESS: A moment today I could treat myself with the same compassion I would offer a friend in a similar situation.

_____

_____

_____

2. Tuesday

PRESENCE: Where I am holding emotion in my body right now, & how I can release it gently today?

INTENTION: The strengths & weaknesses I choose to acknowledge & accept today.

RESOURCES: A positive way my actions can affect others today.

POSITIVES: What went better than I expected today?

CHALLENGES: It was at this turning point today that I started to see progress...

KINDNESS: One kind & loving statement I can say to myself after a difficult day.

---

3. Wednesday

PRESENCE: Feeling into just this present moment, I notice...

___

INTENTION: I will connect back into feeling the present moment during these kinds of stressful/busy times.

___

RESOURCES: A negative belief or behaviour pattern I can observe & gently question today.

___

POSITIVES: What positive outcome today made me feel supported or cared for?

___

CHALLENGES: A wonderful way to recharge during or at the end of a challenging day.

___

KINDNESS: To nurture more self-acceptance in my thoughts tomorrow I will...

4. Thursday

PRESENCE: The sensations I notice in my surroundings—temperature, texture, light.

___
___
___

INTENTION: I can remain calm when I encounter these challenges today...

___
___
___

RESOURCES: Today I can take small and gentle steps towards...

___
___
___

POSITIVES: In what positive way did I handle stress or frustration today?

___
___
___

CHALLENGES: A recent difficulty helped me discover this new strength within myself.

___
___
___

KINDNESS: One negative thought I can let go of tonight, & the positive one I replace it with.

___
___
___

5. Friday

PRESENCE: In this quiet moment of stillness, the thought that is challenging me is...

INTENTION: When I observe this thought without attaching to it, it looks....
(colour/texture/temperature)

RESOURCES: I can bring my resilience & power to these situations today.

POSITIVES: A recent challenge that has helped me grow & that I now feel grateful for.

CHALLENGES: What frustrated me the most about today, & how can I approach it differently next time?

KINDNESS: How did I honour my feelings today, & how can I do that more often?

6. Saturday

PRESENCE: Reflecting on the process of something I am doing, rather than the future outcome reminds me...

_____

_____

_____

INTENTION: I can show myself love today by...

_____

_____

_____

RESOURCES: I can plan to cultivate more peace in these aspects of my day today.

_____

_____

_____

POSITIVES: How did I make a positive impact on someone else's day today?

_____

_____

_____

CHALLENGES: A creative solution I have found for a problem that I will use again.

_____

_____

_____

KINDNESS: A kindness I have given to someone that I will give again.

_____

_____

_____

7. Sunday

PRESENCE: When I imagine stepping back and observing my feelings flow this morning, I can describe it as...

___
___
___

INTENTION: At these times my productivity slows, & but my worth always stays the same.

___
___
___

RESOURCES: What I can offer myself to feel calm & okay, during moments of frustration.

___
___
___

POSITIVES: What experience today made me feel content or fulfilled?

___
___
___

CHALLENGES: How can I approach tomorrow with a growth mindset?

___
___
___

KINDNESS: I embrace these unique qualities in others, & in myself.

___
___
___

R & R

REFLECT
What did you enjoy learning this week, & how did it inspire you?

_____
_____
_____
_____
_____
_____
_____
_____

REFOCUS
What's something new you want to explore or learn next week?

_____
_____
_____
_____
_____
_____
_____
_____

8. Monday

PRESENCE: When I use deep breathing to relax ; my body & mind feel...

INTENTION: My responsibilities today & my intended acts of self-care...

RESOURCES: My instincts are guiding me to....

POSITIVES: Someone I supported or listened to today, & the the gratitude it gives me.

CHALLENGES: An optimistic account of the challenges I have ahead of me.

KINDNESS: A habit or practice I can build that will reinforce positive self-talk in my daily life.

---

9. Tuesday

PRESENCE: A thought I am curious about.

_____
_____
_____

INTENTION: I can nurture peace in my mind today by...

_____
_____
_____

RESOURCES: A strength I can use to help others today.

_____
_____
_____

POSITIVES: What was the best part of my day, & why did it stand out?

_____
_____
_____

CHALLENGES: The first thought I had when faced with a challenge today, & how it shaped my response.

_____
_____
_____

KINDNESS: A thought & an action from today that offered kindness to myself or others.

_____
_____
_____

10. Wednesday

PRESENCE: Feeling present now feels... I will use this resource at these times/breaks/moments today...

INTENTION: Starting the day without putting unnecessary pressure on myself looks like...

RESOURCES: The actions I will take today to maintain my balance & calm...

POSITIVES: An experience today that opened my heart.

CHALLENGES: A fear or doubt, big or small, that I overcame today.

KINDNESS: Who I have shown compassion towards recently, how it felt, & when I can show myself the same.

11. Thursday

PRESENCE: When I bring attention to my breathing right now, I notice...

_____
_____
_____

INTENTION: There is room in my day here... to offer myself this same kindness I would to a friend.

_____
_____
_____

RESOURCES: I have felt confident when... and I can use this feeling to maintain my confidence today when...

_____
_____
_____

POSITIVES: What did I learn today that I am grateful for?

_____
_____

CHALLENGES: When I am patient with myself during challenging moments I notice...

_____
_____
_____

KINDNESS: What is one way I can share kindness with others tomorrow?

_____
_____

12. Friday

PRESENCE: An emotion I am noticing moving through me this morning is...

___

___

INTENTION: My worth feels valued when...

___

___

RESOURCES: I have noted these triggers... I have for this emotion... and I will soothe/calm myself mindfully through them by...

___

___

POSITIVES: A relationship I nurtured in a positive way today.

___

___

CHALLENGES: One way I successfully adapted to a situation today.

___

___

KINDNESS: A self-judgment I noticed today & a self-acceptance I can offer to replace it.

___

___

13. Saturday

PRESENCE: What small detail of this morning can I focus on to bring myself into this moment?

___
___
___

INTENTION: One way I can prioritize my mental & emotional health today.

___
___
___

RESOURCES: These priorities I have today... can be supported by these resources I have...

___
___
___

POSITIVES: Something unexpected today that I am thankful for.

___
___
___

CHALLENGES: A challenge that has given me motivation to improve.

___
___
___

KINDNESS: Something kind I said/did for someone today.

___
___
___

14. Sunday

PRESENCE: Being mindful of the natural world around me now, I feel....

_____
_____

INTENTION: When worry comes my way today, I can do this to detach from it & feel ok.

_____
_____

RESOURCES: These personal strengths... will support the decisions I make today.

_____
_____

POSITIVES: One positive outcome of my actions today.

_____
_____

CHALLENGES: A challenge today that I enjoyed & hope more of the same lie ahead.

_____
_____

KINDNESS: In moments of stress or anxiety, I will offer these kind words in self-talk, & to those around me.

_____
_____

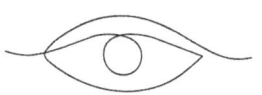

REFLECT

Which of your actions and choices this week are you able to reflect on - both helpful & needing improvement?

_____
_____
_____
_____
_____
_____
_____
_____
_____

REFOCUS

In what way can these reflections positively support the decisions & choices that will present in the week ahead?

_____
_____
_____
_____
_____
_____
_____
_____

15. Monday

PRESENCE: I can observe my attention on the now, pulling it back from future worries or past ruminations feels...

INTENTION: A task I can break down into smaller manageable steps today.

RESOURCES: In my day ahead, I will show myself compassion when...

POSITIVES: What kindness did someone show me today that I appreciate?

CHALLENGES: One way I can stay patient & calm when challenges arise.

KINDNESS: Someone I would like to check in on more regularly.

16. Tuesday

PRESENCE: I have noticed that bringing my attention to the present moment has these greater benefits for me...

_____

_____

_____

INTENTION: An act of self love I can take today.

_____

_____

_____

RESOURCES: Remaining centered in my strength today will allow me to be more open to....

_____

_____

_____

POSITIVES: How did I express or receive love & care today?

_____

_____

_____

CHALLENGES: A problem-solving technique that worked best for me today.

_____

_____

_____

KINDNESS: One thing I want to tell myself tonight to reinforce my sense of worthiness.

_____

_____

17. Wednesday

PRESENCE: When I observe my inner world with curiosity instead of judgment, I notice...

INTENTION: When I make mistakes today, I will offer this kindness to myself...

RESOURCES: An area of my day I will navigate gracefully today.

POSITIVES: One thing about my emotional or mental health that I feel grateful for today.

CHALLENGES: A change I have embraced, even though it felt uncomfortable or difficult at first...

KINDNESS: A flaw I've been hard on myself about, & a softened thought I offer now.

---

18. Thursday

PRESENCE: Soft breath, deep breath, shallow breath: changing my breath, I notice...

INTENTION: What does a balanced, peaceful day look like for me today?

RESOURCES: What I can bring into my relationships & interactions today?

POSITIVES: A difficulty I am grateful I found the strength/courage to push through today:

CHALLENGES: How I can use that strength to approach tomorrow with more confidence:

KINDNESS: One practice I can use to cultivate more self-kindness in the days ahead:

---

19. Friday

PRESENCE: What does being present in conversations with others today look like & sound like?

_____

_____

INTENTION: A compassionate inner dialogue today starts with these words...

_____

_____

RESOURCES: When self-compassion & self-confidence coexist it feels like...

_____

_____

_____

POSITIVES: What I feel the most thankful for today & how I can express that gratitude.

_____

_____

CHALLENGES: A lesson I have learnt that will help me stay positive in the future.

_____

_____

KINDNESS: Even when it's hard, I can speak kindly to myself. These are my fall back words of kindness...

_____

_____

20. Saturday

PRESENCE: Finding stillness in my mind brings me...

INTENTION: To help me approach challenges calmly & with clarity today, I will...

RESOURCES: I acknowledge these personal strengths as I start my day.

POSITIVES: One small thing that I might normally overlook but feel grateful for.

CHALLENGES: The emotions that came up for me at challenging times today.

KINDNESS: One positive thing I can say to myself right now to show kindness.

---

21. Sunday

PRESENCE: As I move or stretch my body this morning, the sensations I notice...

_____

_____

INTENTION: In difficult moments today, I will offer myself compassion by...

_____

_____

RESOURCES: As I challenge myself today by... I will balance in self-care by...

_____

_____

_____

POSITIVES: How did I positively impact someone else's day today?

_____

_____

CHALLENGES: A unique power I have discovered in myself.

_____

_____

KINDNESS: A judgement I chose not to put on myself or someone else today.

_____

_____

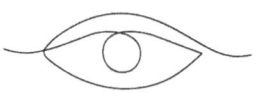

REFLECT
How did you practice kindness toward yourself or others this week?

_____
_____
_____
_____
_____
_____
_____
_____

REFOCUS
Where can you create opportunities to carry that spirit of kindness into the week ahead?

_____
_____
_____
_____
_____
_____
_____
_____

22. Monday

PRESENCE: I notice today, emotionally I am feeling... I can support, move through or prepare for these feelings today by...

INTENTION: When I feel myself comparing myself to others today I will...

RESOURCES: Something unique about me that I will carry confidently into the day.

POSITIVES: One thing about my community that I am grateful for today.

CHALLENGES: My approach to this challenge showed me I am stronger than I thought.

KINDNESS: How can I support myself (and loved ones) with more love & care during challenging times?

---

23. Tuesday

PRESENCE: The words I have to describe being present this morning...

___

INTENTION: Staying within my personal boundaries today looks like...

___

RESOURCES: A mindful practice I can use today & when it will be useful.

___

POSITIVES: How I practiced patience or understanding today, & how it affected my interactions?

___

CHALLENGES: A mistake I have resolved with flexibility or problem-solving skills.

___

KINDNESS: A loving act toward myself (or someone else) I can give tomorrow.

24. Wednesday

PRESENCE: When I use my breath to anchor myself in the present moment it helps...

INTENTION: I can avoid rushing through my day & stay balanced by...

RESOURCES: I can visualise myself in ease & flow at this often challenging time of the day.

POSITIVES: Something I relied on today that made my day easier.

CHALLENGES: A time I learnt to be brave in an uncertain situation.

KINDNESS: A mistake I have let go of and the lesson I have kept.

---

25. Thursday

PRESENCE: My description of a small, often unnoticed detail in my environment.

INTENTION: When I feel my mind starting to overthink... I can tell myself...

RESOURCES: I will use my compassion to support... (someone) through (something) today:

POSITIVES: A small, comforting ritual or routine in my day that I am grateful for.

CHALLENGES: The most empowering part of my day today.

KINDNESS: What encouraging words can I use to support myself tomorrow?

---

26. Friday

PRESENCE: A peaceful moment that quietens the mental noise today feels...

_____
_____

INTENTION: When I start to feel distracted today, I can gently refocus myself by...

_____
_____

RESOURCES: The best way to nurture productivity in my day today will be...

_____
_____

POSITIVES: The joy or creativity I am grateful for today.

_____
_____

CHALLENGES: The positive habits or practices that helped me reduce stress today.

_____
_____

KINDNESS: One thing I can do tomorrow to support my emotional self-care.

_____
_____
_____

27. Saturday

PRESENCE: Breathing mindfully right now feels... & I can use this today when...

———————————————————————————
———————————————————————————
———————————————————————————

INTENTION: I can be kinder to myself when...

———————————————————————————
———————————————————————————
———————————————————————————

RESOURCES: One area of my day where I will try to balance being strong & being gentle with myself.

———————————————————————————
———————————————————————————
———————————————————————————

POSITIVES: Something comforting or reassuring about today that I am grateful for.

———————————————————————————
———————————————————————————
———————————————————————————

CHALLENGES: A moment when I got to practice thinking on my feet.

———————————————————————————
———————————————————————————
———————————————————————————

KINDNESS: Something I can do to make a positive difference to someone else tomorrow.

———————————————————————————
———————————————————————————
———————————————————————————

28. Sunday

PRESENCE: *A common story I notice I am telling myself & a way I am rewriting it.*

INTENTION: *When self-doubt appears today I can release it by...*

RESOURCES: *A challenge coming for me today that I will use as a chance to grow...*

POSITIVES: *Someone or something that made me smile today.*

CHALLENGES: *Something I could & something I could not control today.*

KINDNESS: *When I'm feeling less than perfect, I can show kindness to myself by...*

R & R

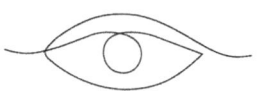

REFLECT
What are you most grateful for having accomplished this week?

_____
_____
_____
_____
_____
_____
_____
_____

REFOCUS
What is one meaningful accomplishment you will focus on achieving next week?

_____
_____
_____
_____
_____
_____
_____
_____

29. Monday

PRESENCE: Savouring this moment... it looks, feels, sounds, tastes, smells like...

INTENTION: My day ahead in self-acceptance & peace could feel...

RESOURCES: I can make confident, aligned choices today when...

POSITIVES: A positive thought or attitude I want to carry with me into tomorrow.

CHALLENGES: One way I can practice positivity when facing a challenge.

KINDNESS: Did I notice my self-talk improving today, & what can I do to continue?

30. Tuesday

PRESENCE: What thoughts are taking up space in my mind, & how can I soften them?

INTENTION: What does a calm & peaceful day look like for me?

RESOURCES: When can I choose to feel strong today?

POSITIVES: A natural beauty or environment around me that I noticed today.

CHALLENGES: A learning experience I had today.

KINDNESS: How can I be more loving toward myself when things are difficult?

---

31. Wednesday

PRESENCE: Tuning in to my body, I notice it needs... today.

INTENTION: Some learning I intend to gather through my day today.

RESOURCES: How can I be my own best supporter today?

POSITIVES: A small, joyful moment I experienced today.

CHALLENGES: What future challenges do I look forward to embracing?

KINDNESS: My imperfections are perfect for me in this way...

2025

REFLECTING ON THE PAST YEAR:

What are three experiences from this past year that made you feel most alive, proud, or at peace? How have they shaped who you are today, and what strengths or insights have you gained from them?

_____
_____
_____
_____
_____
_____
_____
_____

2026

A COMPASSIONATE INTENTION FOR THE YEAR AHEAD:

As you envision the year ahead, what is one intention you'd like to embrace that supports you in being kinder to yourself? How will this intention guide the way you approach challenges, goals, and balance?

_____
_____
_____
_____
_____
_____
_____
_____

Kim ♡

www.ingramcontent.com/pod-product-compliance
Lightning Source LLC
Chambersburg PA
CBHW052130070526
44585CB00017B/1762